To the
BRIDE
with
Love

To the BRIDE with Love

© Oluwakemi O. Ola-Ojo
2010

© OLUWAKEMI O. OLA-OJO

TO THE BRIDE WITH LOVE
First printed by AuthorHouse 6/15/2007
ISBN:978-1-1-4343-0252-6(sc)
Second edition © 2010
ISBN: :978-0-9557898-4-7

All publishing rights belong exclusively to
Protokos Publishers.
Published by Protokos Publishers
P.O. Box 48424
London
SE15 2YL
Website: www.protokospublishers.com

Printed in the United Kingdom.

*All rights reserved under International Copyright Law. Contents and or
cover may not be reproduced in whole or in part in any form without the
express written consent of the Publisher.*

*Unless otherwise stated, all scripture quotations in this book are from
Living Bible [LB], New Revised Standard Version (NRSV) and
the King James Version [KJV] of the Holy Bible.*

Cover design by Prex Nigeria Limited
e-mail: prexng_2000@yahoo.com
Author's photograph by Hill Stanton

To the Bride with Love

CONTENTS

DEDICATION		vi
ACKNOWLEDGEMENT		vii
FOREWORD		viii
PREFACE		x
INTRODUCTION		xii
CHAPTER 1	Basket of Fruits	15
	THE DEAD END	26
CHAPTER 2	Prayer Shawl	29
CHAPTER 3	Jug for Water	39
	WHAT SHALL I RENDER?	47
CHAPTER 4	The Shepherd's Rod	51
CHAPTER 5	Bottle of Perfume	61
	THERE ON THE ROCK	70
CHAPTER 6	Tambourine	73
CHAPTER 7	Beddings and Towels	83
	CAFETARIA	92
CHAPTER 8	Bottle of Olive Oil	97
CHAPTER 9	Bag of Grains	105
	GOD HAS ANOTHER PLAN	113
CHAPTER 10	The Bible and Devotional Book	117
OTHER BOOKS		122
USEFUL ADDRESSES		131

To the Bride with Love

DEDICATION

To brides all over the world.
To my sisters and sisters-in-law.
To all married women of every race, age and colour.

To the Bride with Love

ACKNOWLEDGEMENT

I acknowledge Bolanle Sogunro for her excellent editing, the management and staff of Prex Holdings for the book covers and Protokos Publishers for helping to get this into print and for marketing my books.

To Rev Mrs Yemi Ladokun who spotted my writing skills many years ago and found time to read and write a foreword in spite of her busy schedule, I am most grateful.

To Mrs Bose Olanrewaju, Pastor Mary McCauley, Deaconess Shola Josiah, Deaconess Esther Adeyekun and Mrs Agnes Aniereobi, these wonderful women whose prayer support have enriched my life over the years.

Finally to Evangelist Toun Soetan, my mentor. Her humility and relationship with the Lord has been a wealth of blessing to me.

FOREWORD

By the inspiration of the Holy Spirit, Oluwakemi, the author of this book has been able to dig out the nuggets that will make brides and married women all over the world, of all races, ages and colours succeed in the school of marriage. The content of the book is relevant to a wide range of women. What a remarkable and unique exercise!

How the author has been able to employ ten women from the Old and New Testaments as curriculum contributors for this course on marriage is remarkable. From the very familiar passage on the proverbial woman of noble character (Proverbs 31:10-31), all these women give a perfect picture of what marriage is all about. In the simplicity of this masterpiece, I can also see an imaginary beautiful structure with every letter that spells M-A-R-R-I-A-G-E. In marriage you learn:

M	-	Meekness, Maturity, Motivation, Management
A	-	Appreciation, Accountability
R	-	Reliability, Resourcefulness
R	-	Respect, Regality
I	-	Industry, Integrity, Impartiality
A	-	Availability, Amicability, Adaptability
G	-	Godliness, Graciousness
E	-	Encouragement, Efficiency, Enterprise

To the Bride with Love

The taste of the pudding is in the eating. Get a copy of the book, read it, digest it and share it. Mothers, the book is for you. You will discover where you have erred and how you can give better counsel to your daughters. Pastors, youth leaders, secular and church counsellors and teachers also will appreciate the relevance of the content and use it as reference. The church drama group can positively impact the lives of its membership by dramatizing the content of the book when attendance is good. The book is dedicated to the female world but of great value and benefit to the male world as well.

Dear reader, the bottom line is Jesus God's "Cafeteria" for mankind. In Him only can we discover, choose and enjoy the satisfying, enriching and until-death-do-us-part menu of marriage.

Rev (Mrs) Yemi Ladokun
Current President, Baptist Women's Union of Africa
Executive Director, Women Missionary
Union, Baptist Convention, Nigeria

To the Bride with Love

PREFACE

But as for you, promote the kind of living that reflects right teaching. Teach the older men to exercise self-control, to be worthy of respect, and to live wisely. They must have strong faith and be filled with love and patience. Similarly, teach the older women to live in a way that is appropriate for someone serving the Lord. They must not go around speaking evil of others and must not be heavy drinkers. Instead, they should teach others what is good. These older women must train the younger women to love their husbands and their children, to live wisely and be pure, to take care of their homes, to do good, and to be submissive to their husbands. Then they will not bring shame on the word of God. In the same way, encourage the young men to live wisely in all they do. And you yourself must be an example to them by doing good deeds of every kind. Let everything you do reflect the integrity and seriousness of your teaching. Let your teaching be so correct that it can't be criticized. Then those who want to argue will be ashamed because they won't have anything bad to say about us.

Titus 2:1-8

A wise woman builds her house; a foolish woman tears hers down with her own hands.

Proverbs 14:1

To the Bride with Love

*W*ho can find a virtuous and capable wife? She is worth more than precious rubies. Her husband can trust her, and she will greatly enrich his life. She will not hinder him but help him all her life. She finds wool and flax and busily spins it. She is like a merchant's ship; she brings her food from afar. She gets up before dawn to prepare breakfast for her household and plan the day's work for her servant girls. She goes out to inspect a field and buys it; with her earnings she plants a vineyard. She is energetic and strong, a hard worker. She watches for bargains; her lights burn late into the night. Her hands are busy spinning thread, her fingers twisting fiber. She extends a helping hand to the poor and opens her arms to the needy. She has no fear of winter for her household because all of them have warm clothes. She quilts her own bedspreads. She dresses like royalty in gowns of finest cloth. Her husband is well known, for he sits in the council meeting with the other civic leaders. She makes belted linen garments and sashes to sell to the merchants. She is clothed with strength and dignity, and she laughs with no fear of the future. When she speaks, her words are wise, and kindness is the rule when she gives instructions. She carefully watches all that goes on in her household and does not have to bear the consequences of laziness. Her children stand and bless her. Her husband praises her: "There are many virtuous and capable women in the world, but you surpass them all!" Charm is deceptive, and beauty does not last; but a woman who fears the Lord will be greatly praised. Reward her for all she has done. Let her deeds publicly declare her praise.

Proverbs 31:10-31

INTRODUCTION

Marriage doesn't leave you the same: physically, emotionally, financially, spiritually and sexually. It either enhances or destroys a person. You can hardly remain the same once married.

A popular African adage says 'ile oko ile eko ni' meaning marriage is a learning institution; a school of continual knowledge acquisition, testing, promotions and rewards. It is also the only institution of learning where you receive a certificate before commencing your training. In the Nigerian Baptist Convention many years ago, one of the ceremonies every young lady aspired to have in her honour was the 'Bible Presentation Ceremony' - a beautiful, unique and meaningful ceremony for virgin ladies just before they got married. Apart from being a public celebration of praise to God, it was also an appreciation of integrity, honour, purity and praise to the bride to be. It was usually done during a normal church service. Not only was the bride presented with a Bible as the name of the programme suggested, she was prayed for by chosen Christian married women usually from her congregation with proven track records of successful marriages. They offered her words of encouragement from the Bible or their personal experiences and she was given symbolic gifts to take into her marriage. The gifts usually included cooking pots, cooking spoons, wooden spoon, sweeping brush, dustpan and various other things that she would be using on regular basis - things which could enhance her marriage and items that would remind her of her role in the marriage she was about to enter.

During the traditional marriage ceremony in some African cultures, the bride and groom will call on strategic older members of their families who would offer advice, gifts, blessings and prayers for a successful marriage. Things have changed and will continue to change, but the mystery, the joy, the blessings and challenges of marriage will still make any marriage a learning institution irrespective of affluence, influence or intellect of the couple.

This book has been primarily written for every bride to be as a gift from ten experienced married women in the Bible. Imagine a ceremony in which, you as the bride to be have the privilege of sitting with these women. You hear each of them pray for you and very importantly, give you practical tips for a successful journey which you are about to begin when you say 'I do' whether in a family/traditional setting, marriage registry or Church. This is also a book for the married as the truths shared in it can be applied to their various situations as well.

Each of the women will encourage you from Proverbs 31 quoted above and then go on to share with you tips on what to do or not do, to make your marriage successful. The women will talk to you in the order of their appearance in the Bible. May the Lord guide you and bless you as you read in Jesus' name.

Basket of Fruits

*Fear GOD, and keep His commandments;
for that is the whole duty of everyone.
Ecclesiastes 12:13b.*

Basket of Fruits

You are wondering which of the women in the Bible will be stopping by your place to share her experience with you as you prepare for your wedding. Then comes a knock on the door and you go to open it. Guess who comes in first to wish you well? Mother Eve! As she comes in, she gives you a basket full of assorted fruits and after the warm greetings you both sit and here is what she has to tell you.

Who can find a virtuous and capable wife? She is worth more than precious rubies. She is worth more than precious rubies. Her husband can trust her, and she will greatly enrich his life.

Proverbs 31:10

Congratulations my dear daughter on the life long journey you are about to begin with the love of your husband. Among the many millions of women available, your fiancée has found and chosen you. If you can but take some time to re-examine your life, there is a possibility that you possess some characteristics that made him chose you among the many others. Try to identify those attributes and improve on them with the help of the Lord.

What is your worth in the marriage you are about to go into? It should not be determined in monetary terms; it should be based on what cannot be quantified by any human measure. Will your husband be able to trust you with stories about his failures, secrets, strengths, decisions etc.? Will you be able to protect his interests at all times, in all situations so long as it is not contrary to the Bible? Ask the Lord for help and consciously develop a character that will make your husband fully trust that you will look after his interest in life till God calls you home.

Marriage, as God ordained it, is to be a lifetime covenant and commitment. Know that as long as you are alive, your husband will need your help and vice versa. Your primary assignment to God as a married woman is to your husband and immediate family, ministering to all their spiritual, emotional and physical needs as the Lord empowers you.

My dear -------------------- *(please insert your name)*, my advice to you on this new journey of life that you are about to take is not much. First, please know that you were created and ordained to be a help meet for your husband (Genesis 2:18, 21-25). You are equipped to motivate and bring out the best in him. God has made you strong in your husband's areas of weakness. Be a help meet not a competitor or destroyer of his anointing or destiny.

My daughter, God's words are important and they are to be taken seriously. He knows the end before the beginning so in His kindness, He will warn us or tell us what to do or not do. God speaks to us through His written word (the Bible) and through the Holy Spirit. Spend quality time, daughter, to read and meditate on the Bible yourself; be like the Berean Christians. Take notes and highlight God's instructions as you read. Take seriously whatever He says. Remember that 'God's divine revelation needs no second opinion'. Learn from me my daughter, I listened to the opinion of Satan – the serpent and that became my most costly mistake.

Avoid disobedience for it does not make anyone wise like God or wiser than Him, rather it usually leads to sin which causes all forms of disease, death, separation from God and man. Disobedience is rebellion against authority, which includes that of your husband and God's. The serpent deceived me but I disobeyed God by eating the forbidden fruit. My disobedience, which at that time looked innocent, has brought about so much harm into the world today. My disobedience cost Adam and myself to be driven out of the beautiful Garden of Eden. Separation from God brought other sins including murder, sickness of all types and grades – some curable others incurable even with the latest research and technology. If anything, please avoid disobedience. Be careful, as your sins of today may affect your seeds of tomorrow:

Basket of Fruits

God blesses the people who patiently endure testing. Afterward they will receive the crown of life that God has promised to those who love him. And remember no one who wants to do wrong should ever say, "God is tempting me." God is never tempted to do wrong and he never tempt anyone else either. Temptation comes from the lure of our own evil desires. These evil desires lead to evil actions, and evil actions lead to death. So don't be misled, my dear brothers and sisters.

James 1:12-16

My dear -------------------- *(please insert your name)* watch those you associate with for they can either promote or demote you. Your associates can either make or break you; they can enhance or destroy your marriage; they can hinder you and in turn hinder your husband especially in his God given assignment or call. The saying is true 'show me your friend (associate) and I will tell you your future.' My association with the serpent was the cause of my downfall and that of the human race. Before taking advice from any associate, examine it and be clear on why they are giving you such an advice. Is it to trap you and deceive you into failing and falling or do they genuinely have your interest at heart? Any one who encourages you to disobey God even in the smallest or least instruction is an evil associate whom you have no business relating with. Run away from such a person.

My dear --------------------- *(please insert your name)* learn to focus on what gifts and blessings God has given you rather than on what you haven't been given. A wise person once said when you take what God has not given you, He takes what He has given you. We had the whole garden full of fresh, juicy, lovely fruits but God warned Adam and I not to eat of the fruit of the tree of the knowledge of good and evil. Out of lust, greed and disobedience I wasn't contented any more with all the other fruits and following the suggestion of the serpent I lost my self-control, eat the forbidden fruit and gave some to my husband too. In my sin, I dragged my husband along and caused him too to sin. God hasn't made any rejects. He endows everyone with a gift or talent. Find yours and use it to His glory to bless mankind. Don't lust after or grab other people's gifts.

Know what you feed your husband with physically. Up until you are married, your husband may have been doing his own cooking but with your coming into his life, he may, like many men relinquish most, if not all, his kitchen duties. Then the onus falls on you to fix the family meals. The kitchen in most homes is the department or domain of the woman of the house. I thought the way to show my love to Adam was to feed him with some of the forbidden fruit I had been deceived to eat, as it tasted nice. It was a terrible and costly mistake to Adam and me. Sin will always initially taste nice and feel good but at the end are hatred, guilt, nausea, disgust and fear. Sin is sin; it comes with a price that is usually very costly. Sin is an eye opener that leads to a dead end.

What do you plan to feed yourself, your husband or family – physically, spiritually, financially etc.? Many of the so-called tasty foods (junk foods inclusive) these days are full of sugar, too much salt, preservatives, additives, colourings etc. The outcome is that some of these foods when eaten may make members of your family become unhealthy. Pork and its products, crab, coffee, etc. though very sweet and pleasing to your taste buds may be poisonous to the human body. Carbonated sweet drinks are not only harmful to the teeth and body in general, they are also said to be the cause of some brain tumours. Don't pacify yourself and family members with such foods, drinks and snacks: choose the healthier happier way. There are many good cookbooks out there that will teach you step by step on how to cook a good food/ meal if you do not know how already. Don't just buy books, read and use them.

It is also important to consider what you feed the mind and soul of your husband. If you feed him with lies, deceit, untrue rumour, gossip, anger, bitterness, unhealthy jealousy, sibling rivalry, etc. he will end up less than what and who God created him to be. If care is not taken, you may even be leading him downhill in all ways that may lead to self-destruction. Encourage the priest, man, and king in your husband. Learn to feed him with Godly advice, books, encouragement and motivation that will help bring out the best in him irrespective of any prevailing circumstances.

The 'blame game' is still very much around as when Adam and I first devised it. As you go into this marriage, learn to take full responsibility for your actions or inactions instead of pushing the blame to someone or something else. When confronted by God for our disobedience, my husband blamed me and I blamed the serpent. God however was not impressed by our blame game but pronounced His judgement on us. By the same token, He announced His plan of redemption for mankind. If you will confess your sins and seek the face of the Lord, He is faithful and just to forgive you of all your sins and redeem you from destruction. No sin is too much/big for God to forgive.

Every conception and delivery is by the help and grace of God so learn to seek His face for an appropriate name for your child. Give your children names that will reflect your belief in God. Please don't forget too that you are a co-creator with God (Genesis 4: 1). Watch out and quench on your knees any form of rivalry and jealousy between your children, as it could be destructive. In my family, jealousy made Cain to kill his brother Abel. Please teach and train your children to be one another's keeper. Teach them to fear and love the Lord their creator. Of equal importance is teaching them to give worthy sacrifices unto the Lord.

Finally my daughter, God is able to replace whatever you lose in marriage including children if you will but call upon Him. When God pronounced His judgement against the serpent, I heard Him say my seed would bruise the serpent's head (Genesis 3:14-16). It was a joy for me to know that God will use my seed to destroy the serpent completely. My first pregnancy was delivered in pain but I kept holding on, trusting that the children I will give birth to will someday destroy the serpent. Years passed by and my sons grew old enough to worship the Lord by themselves. God accepted Abel's sacrifice but rejected that of Cain. Cain became jealous of his brother and was angry that Abel's sacrifice to the Lord was accepted. God warned Cain but he did not heed the warning. One day in anger, he lured Abel to the fields and killed him there. Expectedly, God saw it all and banished Cain from His presence.

The loss of our Abel was so devastating and so was the banishment of Cain. I could not imagine that my sin of 'harmless disobedience' could open my seeds to destruction. Both boys who could have crushed the serpent's head were no more available. God had spoken but how would this now be fulfilled? Years later when I least expected it, the Lord visited and blessed my womb, I bore another son whom I named Seth. The good Lord replaced Abel whom Cain had killed (Genesis 4:25- 26). And with Seth came a new and anointed beginning.

Daughter before I take my leave, I will like to pray with you. Let's pray please.

Father I thank you for the life of ------------------ (put your name) that will soon be getting married to one of your sons. Lord, may you help her to take Your words seriously and apply them to every part of her life. Please, Lord, keep her soul and mind from every distraction and disobedience so that her sins of today will not affect her seed of tomorrow. Father, please give her good associates and help her to be one too. Please help her to lovingly feed her husband and family members with those foods and drinks that will not endanger their lives or make them become unhealthy. Lord help her to be mindful of what she ministers to the soul and mind of her husband, encouraging him and not pulling him down, supporting him to obey, rather than disobey You. May there never be rivalry or jealousy among her children in Jesus name. Finally Lord, please give her double blessings for any trouble that she might encounter in this new journey of life. Kindly replace any thing of significance to her, which she may loose along the way in Jesus name I pray with thanksgiving. Amen.

What a wealth of knowledge that Mother Eve left me with plus the basket of fruits. How I wish she could still give me more nuggets for a successful marriage but I am thankful for what she shared with me. I am now more eager to having the other nine women visit me. As I pick each of the fruits to admire I shall try to remind myself of all that she said mainly:

◆ I need to discover my worth, and use it in my marriage.

- God ordained marriage to be a lifetime commitment.
- I should live a trust worthy life.
- God's word or instruction however small or trivia is to be obeyed.
- Disobedience to God is expensive and can open the door to generational problems including death.
- What I feed my husband and family is important to their overall well being, physically, spiritually, emotionally etc. Therefore I should be careful of what I set before them or say to them.
- My ignorant sin of today may wait for my seeds to come before attacking them.
- I must avoid dragging others especially my husband/family into sinful behaviours.
- I should learn to take full responsibility for my actions or inactions instead of pushing the blame to someone or something else.
- Forgiveness and redemption are available from God if I will but confess and forsake my sins.
- The 'blame game' does not help in any married life so I should prayerfully avoid it.
- Every conception is from God and I should learn to acknowledge Him for every conception.
- Only with the help of God can I bring forth.
- Sibling jealousy can be very dangerous; I need to pray such off on my knees in prayer and foster peace among my children.

- My children are to be taught about giving a worthy gift to the Lord.
- God will always fulfil His promises no matter my loss.
- God is able to give me a new anointed beginning and replace whatever I lose in the marriage.

THE DEAD END

It starts like any other useful, straightforward road
It looks so beautiful and very attractive
Very promising is the quality at the beginning
With promising signs to a destination at last.

What an unfortunate mistake to travel on it
What seemed initially attractive and beautiful
What seemed unending and everlasting
Turns out to be just one of the dead ends.

Every sin dear friend is a dead end
For in the end it is full of disgrace and regrets
Full of heartaches, uncertainty and hatred
Full of bitterness, pity and unaccountable loss.

No matter how small or big that sin is
No matter where, when and how it was committed
No matter what excuse we might want to give
It does not remove the sin from being the dead end.

To the Bride with Love

Now is the time to retrace your steps friend
Now is the time to reassess the situation
Now is the time to seek the Lord's face once more
In order that you might not end up in the dead end.

The dead end has nothing to really offer you friend
It has no guarantee, no security nor peace
It has no degree of commitment or improvement
It has no hope for a better future friend.

In your daily walk in life dear friend
Try and watch out for the dead end
Do not be attracted to it or trapped in it
For ultimately it is going to be the dead end.

© O. Ola–Ojo 11.03.92.

Prayer Shawl

Do not worry about anything, but in everything by prayer and supplication with thanksgiving let your requests be made known to God. And the peace of God which surpasses all understanding, will guard your hears and your minds in Christ Jesus.
Philippians 4:6-7

Prayer Shawl

As you are still pondering over the advice Mother Eve gave, there is another knock on your door. 'Who can that be this time' you ask? Then comes in Mother Sarah. Very elderly but exceptionally beautiful. After the pleasant greetings she gives you a beautiful prayer shawl, takes her seat and starts to talk.

> *She will not hinder him but help him all her life. She finds wool and flax and busily spins it. She is like a merchant's ship; she brings her food from afar.*
>
> *Proverbs 31: 11 - 14*

May the Lord help you to be an asset to your husband and not a liability all the days of your life in Jesus' name. May your relationship with your husband enhance his life, career, ministry, and all his endeavours.

May you not hinder him in any way in Jesus name. My sister, watch out for any behaviour and attitude in you which can hinder your husband. These include backbiting, looking down on him, reducing his ego, ignoring his heart cry for help, putting him down consciously and unconsciously, not believing in him and befriending his enemies.

A ship does not sail on a river but on seas and oceans. A merchant ship is primarily for business not for pleasure. Imagine the challenges on the sea yet the ship in most cases does not get damaged but bring all the people and merchandise in it safely to their destination. In spite of life's challenges and uncertainties may you bring good merchandise to your husband and children. May you lay your hands on profitable business ventures through which you can bless God and His works. May God endow you with the supernatural ability to find sustainable businesses and may you not be lazy in all that the Lord will assign you to do in Jesus' name.

Take time to find out in what area(s) of life your husband might benefit from your help and do not hesitate to prayerfully allow God to bless and equip you for the task(s) in Jesus' name. A wise woman once said that the primary duty of a married woman is to look after her husband. Anything that hinders your husband will certainly hinder you as well. It is important that you guard against any form of impediment in your husband's life that may want to attack him through your own behaviour.

My dear ------------------- *(please insert your name)* you need to believe God all the way (not some or most of the way) in all that He has said and will say to you in this new life of marriage. Believe God for He is your Creator and your Maker. He is a Father who loves and does not condemn, who heals and makes whole and does not destroy, who is able to go ahead of you into this venture and at the same time walk along with you all the way. You need to believe God when things are working and when they aren't; when all of His promises seem to be delayed in your eyes and estimation; when it seems He has forgotten you; when the world is mocking and laughing at you. You will need to believe Him for He alone can help you and in Him only is victory and fulfilment.

When God called my husband Abram out of Hur to the Promised Land, he was seventy-five years old and I was about sixty-five. God promised to bless us and make our children numerous as the sand of the sea and the stars in the sky. Years went by without the physical manifestation of this particular promise yet all of our servants and slaves were having children and so were our cattle and chickens. In our home at some point we had over three hundred children born by our slaves and servants but none was ours. The shame and pain in my heart was so much that I had to think of a way out of the situation.

It was popular in those days to give trusted slaves to one's husband to sleep with in order that one might raise children through them. My daughter, be careful in what advice you give to your husband especially in critical times, as not all norms or acceptable behaviour is good or of God. All things are lawful but not all things are helpful or expedient (1 Corinthians 6:12). Remember one who shares your bed with your husband will surely share his heart, emotions, love and desires. My daughter, the fact that it was popular didn't make it suitable for us or acceptable to God for our lives. I didn't consult with God before I advised my husband. In my heart I thought, why do I need to consult God whom I assumed then had either forgotten us or sealed my womb. I gave my slave to my husband as was the order of the day and once she got pregnant she became ill mannered and uncontrollable.

We didn't have the company of the slave's son as I hoped for. Her disobedience and taunting were worse than our barrenness and at some point, I had to tell her to leave with her son. They departed from my family but waited for our promised son to grow up and to torment him even till today. My wrong advice waited for my future seed. In the heat of any matter if you must, then give your husband Godly advice only.

During one of His visitations to my husband long before we had our son Isaac, Jehovah changed our names. My husband, Abram was to be called Abraham –'father of many nations' and I, Sarai was to be called Sarah 'a mother of nations' - our new names were a confirmation of what God promised us (Genesis 17:5,15,16). Sister you may need to ask God for a new name. People may see you and call you names like barren, sick, poor, etc. but God calls you fruitful, mother of many, healed and whole, rich and wealthy, beautiful and solid.

God's timing is always right even though it may not be like ours. He created the world in an orderly fashion; He has everything under His control and has assigned everything created for a specific purpose. Your miracle might seem too late compared with that of your siblings or contemporaries but not only will it come, it will come to fulfil God's divine purpose for the world. In the time you are waiting for your miracle, develop and prepare yourself for it.

Barrenness should not affect your sexual life my dear. Sexual intercourse is the peak of expressed affection between couples. God ordained it first for companionship, intimacy and then for procreation. When people get married they marry without children but God in His mercy brings children along in the marriage and years later, if all goes well, the children will leave the family and once again the couple will be by themselves. Have fun and don't deny yourself or your husband of sex on account of barrenness or delayed fertility. Only God knows which of those intimate fellowships will end up in procreation. I was almost ninety years old when God visited us again and announced that I would nurse a child for my husband. It was hard to believe that an old lady like me could have pleasure again in having sex with my husband. However we obeyed the Lord and what seemed impossible when we were younger came to pass in our old age when by all human standards it was over for us.

Between the promise of God for our lives and its manifestation there is always a period of waiting. Once you have heard God on any matter please hang in there with Him for He speaks no careless words. His promises are pure like silver seven times refined (Psalm 12:6). In our case we waited a quarter of a century – 25 years! But it came to pass. I had a son for father Abraham after I had humanly passed menopause and "menostop". Daughter though the vision God gives you tarries; I encourage you to wait on Him for it shall surely come to pass (Habbakuk2: 3).

Be hospitable for you could sometimes entertain angels unawares. Busy as you may be my dear, everything has its day of reward including being good to strangers. Entertaining guests, especially relatives, in-laws, friends, the unexpected traveller or even our enemies, could be very challenging for any woman but it could also be an opening for some blessings, which would not have come otherwise. Make your home a place of peace, protection and provision for as many needy people that you meet. There will always be some sort of challenge you will face at one time or the other in marriage but my daughter, learn to take your eyes away from your challenges. Fix them on the Lord and seek for ways of helping others in need. Sacrificially sow your seed of giving and hospitality especially when it is not that convenient for you. You never can tell which will bring the desired result (Ecclesiastes 11:6).

One sunny day, my husband saw three men approaching and he quickly asked them to stop by and eat with us. Preparing a whole lamb and bread without prior notice, as you would imagine was not an easy task but I obeyed my husband. Little did I realise that those men were angels on a mission to Sodom and Gomorra. More importantly, I didn't know that they had the rhema (revealed) word for our child's conception and delivery. Please so long as it is not contravening God's word or will, daughter, learn to obey your husband even when you have not been adequately briefed about his instructions. My obedience in cooking at short notice and setting up the table paid off.

Whatever the challenges you may face in your marriage please be reassured that God always brings 'Isaac' in spite of all trials. Isaac means laughter and God will make you laugh over the follies of your enemies and delays in Jesus' name. Your miracle will not be hidden but it will be made public in a way that all your enemies will run back to you and rejoice with you whether they like you or not. I guarantee you that God's fulfilled promise always brings laughter irrespective of the delays and the odds you might have passed through. The Bible says that weeping may go on for the night but joy comes in the morning (Psalm 30:12). Daughter of Zion, God will certainly visit you and bring your Isaac in Jesus' name.

Please let's pray together.

Father, God of my husband Abraham, of our son Isaac and our grandson Jacob, it is with joy that I present your daughter ------------------ (insert your name here) before you this day in the name of Jesus. I thank you for bringing her to such an honourable position of marriage. I humbly ask that your presence will be real to her all through the journey especially at times when she might be lonely due to circumstances beyond her control. I pray that your promises for her will not be delayed to the extent of her doing things she ought not to do; saying things she ought not to say; or being where she ought not to be. Help her not to give her husband or family the wrong advice in Jesus' name. Equip her Lord to give her husband Godly advice only. Please, give her the strength, wisdom and resources to make her hospitable to all that come her way and are in need of help. Father, give her reasons daily to laugh a laugh of victory and may your joy and laughter not depart from her in Jesus' name.

She bids you farewell and you sit to think about her gift for you and what you learnt from her mainly:
- I should be an asset in my marriage not a liability.
- I am to prayerfully avoid being a hindrance to my husband.
- I should lay my hands on profitable business.
- I must believe God all of the way.
- I should be careful and mindful in what advice I give my husband especially at critical times.
- Wrong advice can wait for my future seed.
- I may need to ask God for a new name.
- God's promises for my life will surely come at HIS own appointed time by His own method and for His own ordained purpose.
- I should enjoy sexual life irrespective of the odds.
- Obedience to God always pays and He will give me my own 'Isaac'.
- I should wait patiently and purposely on God.
- I should be hospitable at all times.
- I should obey my husband.

To the Bride with Love

MY PERSONAL NOTES

Jug for Water

A generous person will be enriched, and one who gives water will get water.
Proverbs 11:25

To the Bride with Love

Jug for Water

"Wow! That was powerful", you say then you hear a knock.

As you open the door, in comes a very pretty middle aged woman. As you say hello, her response is "I am Rebecca and I am here to congratulate you and encourage you on the journey of life that you are about to take". She gives you a beautiful jug for water. You both sit down.

She gets up before dawn to prepare breakfast for her household and plan the day's work for her servant girls.
Proverbs 31:15

Getting up before dawn gives you the opportunity to spend some quality time with the Lord before the family awakes. At the same time, you are able to plan for the day not only for yourself but also for the other members of your household. Failure to pray, to prepare and to plan can be disastrous. Learn to set your family out for the day with prayers and a good breakfast if eating is not contraindicated (i.e. provided the doctor has not placed your family member on a special or strict diet) and they are not fasting. Working outside the home or doing a corporate job is no excuse for not making sure that your family eats good meals. Carbonated drinks, coffee and unhealthy food may harm the health of your family. Only God knows what any day would hold, but with a tummy full of a balanced diet, members of your household can have a good start to the day. Be mindful of what you feed your husband, children and anyone else living with you, be it an uncle or aunt, au pair, house help or guest.

Without vision, my people perish. So says God. With vision comes planning on how to make the vision clearer. Rich or poor, learned or not, everyone has twenty-four hours to spend each day. Any unused time cannot be reserved, kept or transferred to another person. One of the success tips for the lady of the house is to identify the areas of needs in her family, prioritise what work is to be done, assign who is best for which job and ensure that the task is properly completed. In other words, be a woman of strategic planning on a daily basis at home, at work and outside your home. How time flies is a popular saying. However, time doesn't have to fly if you prayerfully and strategically plan, and wisely use the time available to you on daily basis.

My dear --------------- *(please insert your name)* it is a privilege that I Rebecca have been chosen to share with you some of my marital experiences trusting God to use them to bless you in your forthcoming marriage.

Difficult as it may be to accept, be clear about this that curses and blessings run in families. Don't be surprised that you will discover some very challenging things that are peculiar to your family or husband's family but prayer is the key to overcoming every family challenge or curse. My parents in-law suffered from infertility and in their old age gave birth to my husband who was the heir not only to my in-law's wealth but also to God's promises given by covenant to my father in-law (Genesis 12:1-3). Blessed and wealthy as we were, my husband and I, like his parents, had problems conceiving for many years after our marriage though we were both virgins when we married. This was a great challenge that our wealth and position could not resolve.

To be born or married into wealth is great and good but it is limited. Most of the good things of life are not ones that you can buy. For example, you cannot buy good health, children, peace and joy. Where your position and wealth may fail, prayers will not. My husband prayed and interceded and twenty years into the marriage God blessed us with a set of twins. Be it curses or challenges ahead, daughter, please learn to intercede and exercise faith for I can tell you it works. Nothing should be too small or too big for you to discuss with God. He cares and is able to meet your needs no matter what they are.

Encourage your husband to be open to God and do not forget to always pray for and with him. It is very important to do so as most, if not all, of the decisions on where the family should or shouldn't be rest on him. It is one thing to ask God for a child and another thing to carry the pregnancy. Learn to pray through every pregnancy, easy or complicated as it may be. In my days there was no ultrasound scanning to check any pregnancy or to peep into the womb like today. However, good as an ultrasound scan examination may be, showing you the physical features of the unborn baby, the purpose and destiny of that child are only known to God the Creator and sustainer of that pregnancy.

Don't forget to seek the will of God concerning each of your children biological or adopted. I felt a struggle within me while I was pregnant and when I could take it no more; I prayerfully took the matter to God in prayers. In His infinite mercy, God heard me and told me about the pregnancy. God has not, and will not change, what He did for others including me; He will do for you too in Jesus' name.

Knowing the destiny of each of your children before birth is very rewarding when the information is positive but even so you still need to continuously intercede for the timely manifestation of such destiny. When the privileged information is not good, I believe you can still change it as you pray and intercede for the children. Information about each child should not affect your affection or love for that child or your other children. There is a wise saying that anything that is good needs prayers to sustain it and anything that is bad needs prayers to correct or change it to good.

No two pregnancies or children are the same. Daughter, take time to know each of your children, appreciate their individuality and by all means avoid favouritism. Esau was my husband's favourite while Jacob was mine. Nothing ruins the family relationship or fuels sibling rivalry as favouritism. Rather than have a favourite child, if you must, have the favourite in different aspects, e.g. the best child in house cleaning, completing school homework, caring about others and so on. Favouritism can blind the eyes of parents to the good traits of their other children. Favouritism can make the unfavoured child angry, disobedient and rebellious. The favoured child gets exposed and becomes vulnerable to the other children. In my family, Jacob lived in the fear of death from Esau for many years until God changed his name in a fierce contest. Learn to make your home a resting place not a wrestling ring.

Watch the names you give to your children for as a person's name is so he or she is. We named our second son Jacob meaning grabber, trickster and so he was for many years of his life. Looking back now we should have given him a name that would reflect God's mission for his life or destiny not a name that showed how he was born. That was a mistake on our part so, daughter watch out for this.

Learn to launch each of your children into their destiny. Should the Holy Spirit reveal the mission or ministry of your child to you, don't only pray about it, prayerfully stir the child towards that destiny. Every child conceived is on God's agenda for the world, and I challenge you as the mother to find out from God what purpose your child was created for. At the same time, as you prayerfully watch your child, you will soon learn what areas the child leaning towards. For instance, is the child always reading or writing, or drawing or being extremely caring and kind toward others? This will guide you in the direction the child should be going.

Having heard from God about our twins, I took it upon myself to ensure that Jacob not Esau received the first born's blessing, I also ensured that he married from my brother's family not a strange woman. I felt that in order to protect Jacob's life it was important that he moved away form Esau so I carefully organised for him to go far away to my brother. One word of caution though, launching your child into his or her destiny could be costly in terms of what you may have to give up and sometimes you may not even live long enough to see the child's future being fulfilled. No matter what, do not add any form of curse to your life or that of your family members. I promised to take any curses that might arise from Jacob taking Esau's blessing; unfortunately I did not live to see Jacob return from my brother's years later.

Finally, be a peacemaker not a peace breaker especially among your children. It is sinful and evil to play 'divide and rule' among people especially your children. I gave Esau's best outfit that he kept with me to Jacob to wear to deceive their father. That did not make me popular with Esau, on top of other things. My sister, please avoid betraying the trust of any of your children and family members.

I guess it's time for me to allow others to speak to you but before I go shall we pray together please?

> *Dearest Father, the God of my father in-law, of my husband and family, how privileged I am to be called upon to share some of my experiences with Your daughter who is just about to enter into the institution of marriage.*

Your word says we have been removed from the curse of the law so Father I ask that in Jesus' name, You will give her victory over any known or unknown curse that may be plaguing her husband and her family before now. Lord, please grant Your daughter the fruit of the womb without undue delay in Jesus' name. Please grant her the grace to intercede before, during and after each conception. Help that she might cooperate with You and the Holy Spirit in bringing up her children in Your love and fear. Help her Lord not to destroy her own family by having favourites or showing favouritism among her children. May she help and support her husband all the days of his life and not connive with people to deceive him in Jesus name. Lord, establish each of her children for Your name's sake in Jesus' name we pray with thanksgiving.

You see her off to the door and return to admire the beautiful water jug. As you are doing so you ponder on what you learnt from her talk mainly:

- I should learn to prayerfully plan and prepare my family daily.
- I should feed my family with balanced meals.
- Curses and blessings run in each family. Prayer is the overcoming key in both situations.
- Nothing is impossible with prayers.
- I should pray before, during and after each conception.
- I should take time to pray for each of our children's destiny.
- I should take time to appreciate and know each of our children.

- I should choose names that will reflect God's destiny for each child.
- I should avoid showing favouritism to any of our children.
- I should avoid betraying the trust of any of our children.
- I should make our home a resting place not a wrestling ring.
- I should not connive with others to deceive my husband or children.
- I should launch each child into his/her God ordained destiny.
- I should be a peacemaker not a peace breaker.
- I must avoid adding any form of curse to my family or myself.

WHAT SHALL I RENDER?

What shall I render to you my Lord?
For making me wonderfully complex
With ears to hear, nose to breathe,
Mouth to eat, eyes to see,
Legs to walk and hands to hold and write.

What shall I render to You my Lord?
For creating me in Your own very image
For making me Your child through Jesus Christ
For cleansing me from my sins and guilt through His blood
For giving me life in abundance through His love.

What shall I render to You my Lord?
For giving me fresh air to breathe
For giving me water to drink, cook and wash
For giving me all kinds of fruits and food to eat
For giving me good health to enjoy them all.

What shall I render to You my Lord?
For my loving and caring parents
For my understanding brothers and sisters
For my very nice neighbours and friends
For my tolerant colleagues at work.

To the Bride with Love

What shall I render to You my Lord?
For my faithful and loving husband
For my hardworking and understanding wife
For my God fearing and obedient children
For my caring and pleasant in-laws.

What shall I render to You my Lord?
For the clothes, which keeps me warm?
For the shelter in which I reside and I'm protected
For the sun and moon which gives me light
For the rain which gives me water?

What shall I render to You my Lord?
For all these blessings told and untold
I will forever give You my thanks
Telling others about Your wonderful love
I will priase You with all I have.

© O. Ola- Ojo 10/11/88.

To the Bride with Love

MY PERSONAL NOTES

The Shepherd's Rod

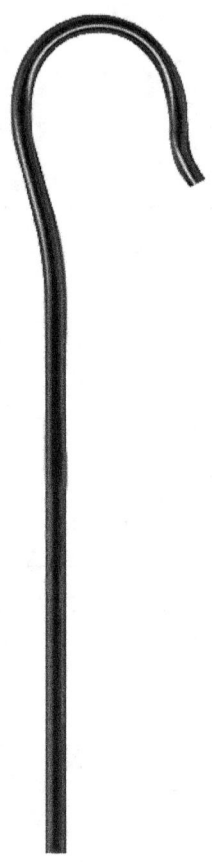

A good wife is the crown of her husband, but she who brings shame is like rottenness in his bones.
Proverbs 12:4

The Shepherd's Rod

Just as you sit down sipping your favourite fruit juice, there is another knock on the door. Opening the door there is yet another pretty woman holding in her hand what look like some idols, a shepherd's staff and rod. She gives you the shepherd's staff and rod. Before you can think of what to say, she says, "Hello, I am Rachel. I thought I should stop by to wish you well in your forthcoming marriage". You allow her to come in. She sits down and you offer her a drink, which she accepts. Here is what she says to you.

> *She goes out to inspect a field and buys it; with her earnings she plants a vineyard. She is energetic and strong, a hard worker. She watches for bargains...*
> *Proverbs 31:16-18a*

Someone once said, *"See before you touch, touch before you smell, smell before you taste, taste before you eat all to avoid food poisoning"*. There is wisdom in inspecting a field or project before fully committing yourself to it. As this woman was an investor so may the good Lord show you the best ways of investing your time, talents and wealth as a married woman in Jesus' name.

The wise woman above uses her earnings wisely planting a vineyard, which in time will produce fruits, seeds and drinks. Wherever you are lacking in strength physically, emotionally, financially, spiritually or in any other way, may the Good Lord give you His strength so that you may do all that He has for you to do in this marriage. To make your marriage successful you will need to work at it, prayerfully giving it your best shot. A wise woman builds her home (Proverbs 14:1a). What is worth doing at all is worth doing well. Aim, with the Lord on your side, to be hard working even in your marital life.

Learn to watch out for bargains and make the best use of them. That something is a bargain doesn't necessarily mean it is second hand or imperfect. Many stores have seasons of bargains sometimes to clear their warehouse in preparation for the next climatic season, sometimes to make room for their new consignment or if people are not buying in the quantity they projected for. To get good bargains, you will have to exercise a good degree of self-control, self-discipline, delayed gratification, prayerful planning and money saving. In this part of the world (Britain) if you know how to wait and which shops and outlets to look out for, you could save a lot of money on your purchases. Many shops have seasonal sales that could sometimes be ridiculously low. At periods like post Christmas, Easter and bank (public) holiday sales you can plan and buy things, rather than spend loads of money purchasing the same items a few weeks earlier. Bedding, furniture, kitchen measured and fitted, electrical wares etc. are periodically on sale. In some African nations where grains are seasonal, you can plan and buy such grains when they are in season and cheap and store them like Joseph did in Egypt (Genesis 41:44-49). Those grains can sometimes last till the next harvest season if well preserved. With God's wisdom and His strength you will make it in your marriage.

My dear -------------------- *(please insert your name)* I feel so honoured to be asked to share some of my marital experiences with you ahead of the journey you are about to embark upon.

My marriage started in a rough and painful way. From the moment Jacob and I set eyes on each other we fell in love. Jacob served my dad for seven years so that we could be married but on what was meant to be my wedding night, my dad gave my older sister - Leah to be married to Jacob, as it was our custom. I was deeply hurt and a week later I was allowed to marry Jacob on the condition that he would work for my dad for another seven years first.

Instead of being the first and only wife of Jacob, I became the second wife. Though much loved by our husband in every respect, I just could not conceive, even for an hour but my sister was having babies. I became jealous of Leah and was very competitive in an unhealthy manner. In the spirit of jealousy, I gave my maid Bilhah to our husband to lie with and I named the children she bore Dan and Naphtali. My dear -------------------- *(please insert your name)* in your marriage avoid jealousy, as it is a deadly sin.

I once confronted our husband saying, *"Give me a child or I die"* (Genesis 30:1). That wasn't a good thing to say neither did it reflect my trust in our husband's God as the provider and giver of life. Should you have some delays in conceiving, avoid jealousy and saying the wrong things for I can tell you now that delay is not denial. Thank God for and appreciate your husband's love for you that is not dependent on whether or not you have children. I later learned to call on God and in His own time He heard my cry and gave me a son whom I named Joseph saying may the Lord grant me another son.

A delayed child often is a unique child. In the calendar of the family, Church, and world events, every child has a role to play. Rejoice when there is a delayed conception and hold on to God. Rest assured that God will not only hear and answer you, that child that took so long to come is going to have a strategic assignment if you will but teach and show him or her the ways of the Lord. Who could have guessed that my 'delayed-in-arriving' Joseph would be mightily used of God to save our family, race and the world? While I was thinking that God had forgotten me, little did I realise that He was on my case. I assure you that when it seems your prayers are unanswered by God, He is actually working on your case behind the scenes you are looking at.

I was more physically beautiful than my older sister Leah but I lacked her patience and Godly character. My dear ------------------ (please insert your name) physical beauty is vain without Godly character. It does not matter what you physically look like, try and work on your character as that will hold you longer and get you blessed more than your outward appearance will (important as that may also be in your marriage).

In many cultures, once you are married, what your husband has automatically becomes yours; but even so please don't take his things without telling him especially when he is around. Don't help yourself to other people's belongings without their approval. Be honest in your dealings and hide nothing from your husband especially in terms of each newly acquired item.

I stole my father's idols, without his knowledge or that of my husband. Stealing is very bad and it is against God's commandment that says thou shall not steal (Exodus 20:15). My dad discovered the family idols were missing and he chased after us. When he finally caught up with us, he accused my husband of stealing the idols. Jacob knew he didn't steal them and he trusted the members of his family not to steal. What he didn't know was that I was the culprit. In the integrity of his heart and character, Jacob unknowingly pronounced a curse on whoever stole the idols. I sat on my donkey with the idols properly concealed in it and pretended that I was having a menstrual period. I was able to hide my sin of stealing from everybody but God saw it and I knew it.

My dear ------------------ *(please insert your name)* whatever you do, please avoid a curse from your husband or father as it can be very dangerous. Both men have a responsibility over you as a wife or child. To avoid been laughed at, or reprimanded I couldn't tell anyone that the missing idols were with me. Equally,

I felt that my dad stole my husband from me and gave my older sister to Jacob instead of me at the end of seven years; so I felt justified in my own eyes to steal my father's idols. Perhaps, if I did tell my husband and, or dad, I would have been forgiven for stealing the family idols. Dad could also have neutralised the curse. Good or bad, no matter your motive, please avoid being cursed. You might be able to conceal your sins before man but I tell you it will be well exposed to God.

There may be things that, unknown to your husband, you have picked from your parent's home, which could deter your peace, joy or good health if carried into your marriage. Those things might include physical items like jewellery or property and non-physical things like attitudes. May the Lord open your eyes to identify such contraband items and willingly dispose of them before you enter into this marriage in Jesus' name.

The curse for stealing those useless idols was a death penalty. Nothing 'kills' as fast as sin. It causes all kinds of deaths - physical, spiritual, emotional, financial, social and so on. Please avoid sinning, as it is a sure route to death. The curse did catch up with me later as I was in labour with Benjamin; I never lived to breast-feed him or bring him up [please note that I am not saying that every death at childbirth is due to a curse]. Curses, if not dealt with, will come back and attack the person to whom it was addressed especially if you are in the wrong. I ended up being buried along the road unlike our other ancestors including my sister Leah who were buried in Father Abraham's cave.

Perhaps, as I am speaking to you now the Holy Spirit is reminding you of certain sins that could mar your marriage or cut your life short, do not panic or fear. Jesus has paid in full, the price of your sin(s). All that you need to do is for you to just come to Him confessing and repenting of it (them). In your own words just spend the next few minutes sorting this out with God or you may prefer to say this prayer:

> *Dear God, I thank you for reminding me of the following sin(s) -- ----------------------------------- (please list them), which I now realise could mar my forthcoming marriage or cut my life short. Lord, I am sorry for committing them. Against You oh Lord have I sinned and to You Lord have I run to ask that You please have mercy on me a sinner. I repent of my sin(s) and I ask that You forgive me in Jesus' name. I believe in my heart that Jesus Christ has paid for my sins, past, present and future. Every curse associated with my sin(s), I neutralise with the blood of Jesus. I have been set free from every curse as my Lord paid for them in full by His death. I ask You Lord in Your mercy for the infilling of the Holy Spirit so that with His help, I can live a victorious life becoming all that You have ordained me to be in Jesus' name I pray with thanksgiving. Amen.*

If you can, please return all the stolen physical items like the jewellery or property or at least inform the owners of such.

I'm sure you feel better now after that prayer. Believe that God has heard you and has indeed cleansed you from all unrighteousness. Therefore don't allow the devil to come and haunt you in future with the memory of your forgiven sins. When God forgives, He also forgets.

My dear ------------------, *(please insert your name)* thank you for welcoming me and giving me the drink but shall we pray before I leave.

> *Dear father, the God of my husband and our forefathers, I thank You that I have been chosen to be among those who will encourage Your daughter. Father in the name of Jesus; please help her not to have any form of strife with anyone in her home. May you multiply her and make her fruitful in all her endeavours including giving her, and in your on time, children that are strategically positioned to turn the world round for Jesus. May she never steal from her father or husband or do anything that will put a curse on her in anyway. Help your daughter to be truthful to her husband and family in Jesus' name.*
>
> *Lord, may she have pregnancies and labours free from complications in Jesus' name. May she safely give birth to her babies and grant her good life and good health to take care of her children in Jesus' name. Thank You Lord for answered prayers in Jesus' name we have prayed with thanksgiving. Amen.*

She left you a few minutes ago yet you are still wondering if the idols she was holding were the ones she stole from her dad. You are equally pondering on what you learnt from her marriage mainly:

- I should invest my time, talent and wealth wisely.
- I should prayerfully build my home.
- I should have and exercise self-control, self discipline and delayed gratification.
- I should buy at bargains when and where possible.
- I must avoid jealousy.
- Delays that are inevitable are designed for God's Glory.
- Should I experience delay, I must learn to pray for patience and Godly character.
- A delayed child is often a unique and strategic child.
- I should pay attention to my outward and inward appearances.
- I must not steal and I should avoid concealing events and issues from my husband.
- I must avoid being cursed by those who have authority over me.
- Justified curses can still kill today if not revoked.
- I must pray against complicated pregnancy or and labour.

Bottle of Perfume

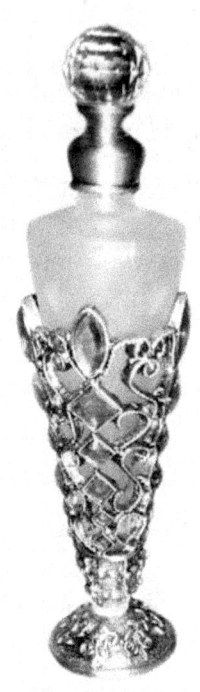

> *But you are a chosen race, a royal priesthood, a holy nation. God's own people, in order that you may proclaim the mighty acts of Him who called you out of darkness into His marvellous light.*
> 1st Peter 2:9.

Bottle of Perfume

Next comes a gentle knock on the door. The woman at the door has with her a bodyguard, a eunuch. She is dressed in royal robes and she is wearing a crown and what a beauty! – I couldn't avoid observing these and commenting on them. As we sat down to eat some fruits, the eunuch came in again asking if she was okay. She gave me a bottle of expensive perfume as my wedding present. *"Who is this woman"?* I began to ask myself. As if she could read my thoughts she said, "I am Queen Esther and I am here to talk to you before your coming wedding."

Her lights burn late into the night. Her hands are busy spinning thread, her fingers twisting fiber.
Proverbs 31:18b-19

In every twenty-four hours there's daytime and night time. Night time could be as long as the daytime. To be safe at night we need light to see; remember the story of the ten virgins? Have the Holy Spirit in you always and He will keep you safe all night. Make your home safe twenty four seven. Let your life be a beacon to many others around you. To be successful in marriage you need to be hard working.

Take time to find out your God-given talents and abilities, take time to develop and use them to the maximum. Whatever your hands find to do, do it very well to bless others and get some profit as well. For some, their nighttime is as productive as their daytime, if not more. If by nature you can work at night, then use it creatively and productively; however try and rest during the day. God loves us to rest too.

My dear ---------------- *(please insert your name)* I was left as an orphan at a very early age and was adopted by my uncle Mordecia. By my Jewish background I wasn't qualified to marry the king but God Himself ordained that my tears of orphanhood be dried. And of all the suitable women, I was chosen to marry the king and be crowned the queen of the vast land. That same God has ordained and allowed you out of numerous other suitable women to soon be married to that man. Your background should not deter you from becoming who God has ordained you to be especially in your husband's home. For any woman, marriage marks a new beginning upon which you can build a glorious future irrespective of your background or experiences to date.

Before going to spend a night with the king, each one of us chosen women was worked on. We had six months of treatment with oil and myrrh and the next six-month's treatment was with sweet spices and perfumes (Esther 2:12). We were also taught many things including palace ethics. May I ask you what sort of preparation you've had or are now having before going into this marriage? If spending a night with the king could demand this much of work and attention to detail what sort of preparation have you had or are you having before you say, *"I do, so help me God"*?

As you go into this life-long relationship, prepare yourself for your husband – inside and outside. Spend quality time in prayers and studying the word of God. Read good books on marital life especially by Christian authors. Read autobiographies of people with successful marriages. Prayerfully invest in yourself qualities and traits that would enhance your relationship with your husband and future family. Pay close attention to practical details too.

Running the home affairs (cooking, washing, shopping, etc.) is mostly in the portfolio of women in many cultures. Please take time to learn in the areas you are lacking before your marriage, if possible. Your physical appearance is equally important. Having a regular and daily bath or shower is good for your skin. Cleanliness, they say, is next to Godliness. Be careful about what perfume you wear as this may attract or repel your husband. Please do not neglect your outward appearance or inner character after your marriage. Above all live your life as a fragrance that will attract others to Jesus Christ and bless God.

Being married to king Ahasuerus required among other things that I should organise and host parties. Certain qualities might be required of you as the Mrs. of a person in your husband's position or career. For example, to be a doctor or medical personnel's wife, you will need to learn to be empathetic, caring and kind, especially to those whose health may not be as good as yours.

You should also live knowing that your husband might often be called out in the night to save other people's lives. If you marry a sales person or marine engineer you must be prepared for periods when you will be alone without the physical presence of your husband perhaps for days, weeks, or months. Certainly, you will need to learn how to exercise self-control especially in keeping yourself solely for your husband while he is away. You may also need to be able to handle some do-it-yourself (DIY) tasks around the home. If you marry a minister of the Word, you would need among other things to learn to joyfully and trustingly share your husband with the Church, be discrete about personal information that might come your way, be hospitable, prayerful, caring and loving even to the unlovable. If you marry an ambassador, you will need to be hospitable, outgoing, and up-to-date in current affairs, discrete and diplomatic.

Marriage is not only about getting your husband to love you and give to you, it is also about knowing what he likes and giving it to him so long as it doesn't offend God. I believe that one of the reasons that I was chosen to become the queen was because I sought for and took the advice of the eunuch on what to wear on my night with the king. The eunuch knew the king and what was more likely to appeal to him better than I did at that time. Your parents and your husband's parents, siblings, in-laws, close friends and associates can help you with this if you do not know already. Talk with them and they will help you to understand your husband better e.g. why he has what fears, what are his favourite foods, sports etc. Go out of your way to meet the needs and likes of your husband in every area including the way you dress (so long as it is not ungodly). That will not only make your husband's heart attuned to you, it will likely make him shower more of his love and affection on you.

The Holy Spirit knows your husband very well too. He will tell you and help you in understanding and looking after him as you humbly seek His face.

Daughter, don't forget your family or root after you are married. Seek for their comfort and bless them as often as you are in the position to do so. There is an old African adage that says that a river that forgets its source will soon dry up. Remembering your roots is not conditional on whether your parents or family invested in you or not. Be a blessing to them. In addition to parents and family, whoever God has used in your life especially to direct and support you should be appreciated and honoured. There might be times when you need to be discrete about your background and who you are. Be wise and take Godly counsel.

There is an assignment for you in your marriage - prayerfully find it and fulfil it with the help of God. Be obedient to God and heed wise counsel. Be sensitive so that you will know when God reveals any impending dangers or blessings to you. When He does, please intercede, fast if need be, and warn the person(s) concerned if possible.

There may come times when you have overwhelming challenges which you either can't discuss with your husband or agree with him over. For example if your husband's close relation or friend is ruining your home, you might need others to pray along with you before you confront or discuss the issue with your husband. But remember that a well-fed man in an atmosphere of love and peace is more likely to meet your demands than otherwise. Prayerfully, carefully and tactfully get rid of bad influences on your husband. Whatever his calling, please be your husband's number one intercessor. Ask God to keep away from him wayward people and the likes of destructive Haman whose self interest was to destroy lives using the king's authority as a cover up for achieving such destruction.

Daughter, marriage is not only about sexual relationship or cuddles. There may be times when due to various duties or challenges you both cannot find time for such intimacy. For about three months in our marriage the king didn't ask for me. The tradition in those days was that nobody could go into the king's presence without being called for and that included me even though I was the crowned queen. During the three months that the king didn't send for me, a serious problem developed with my race that needed the king's attention. I sent word to my people that they should pray and fast with me to seek the face of the Lord for what to do.

It was in this period of prayer and fasting that God showed me what to do and with His help and favour, my entire race was delivered. Daughter, in your marriage watch out for matters that will require your prayer and fasting. Seek God's face for a day or more before you present delicate matters to your husband. Learn from me and I tell you, once you do your part, God in heaven will back you up and you will get your desired outcome in Jesus' name. Unlike my husband the king whom you could only see upon invitation, our heavenly King, the primary lover of our souls, allows us to invite ourselves into His glorious presence any time, anywhere and for any reason. The Bible tells us to come into His presence just as we are, with our burdens, praise and worship. We can enter His presence in our times of need without the fear of His rejection or a death sentence.

To appear before the king, after our fasting and prayer, God gave me the wisdom to go before him in my royal outfit – one he loved. I humbled myself before him and asked him to come for a meal with Haman the traitor. In your marriage, take time to look your best for your husband especially at crucial times. Yes, we as women tend to have more words to say than men do but be humble and gentle with your husband. Prayerfully choose the right place, atmosphere and moment to talk to him if you aim at getting positive results especially in a difficult situation. In the same way, you must learn to appear before God your maker in the best attitude: that of reverence, praise, worship, adoration and humility.

Finally, if you were given the chance to save your family or defend your race, what would you do? Use every opportunity to preserve, protect and promote the life of others especially the underprivileged and those of the household of faith. Today I'm still being celebrated in the land of Israel and worldwide for the help I rendered to save my race. When you are no more, will people be able to celebrate your life?

I can see it's time for me to go now and allow someone else to talk to you but before then, may we pray together please?

Father, in the name of Jesus Christ, I thank You for Your daughter who You are leading by Your grace into the institution of marriage. Lord, please grant her the courage to work on herself, thus enriching her life within and outside with qualities that will make her life more acceptable and profitable to her husband. Lord, grant her the wisdom on how best to eliminate her enemies and satanic threats as she waits upon you in prayers and fasting. Help her as a married woman to be a defender of the hopeless, helpless and weak and may she use every opportunity available to her in this cause in Jesus' name I pray with thanksgiving. Amen.

Wow! What an impressive advice you say to yourself and how you wish there was more time to spend with her. As you are putting the bottle of perfume with your other gifts you try to recapture what you learnt from the queen:

- Marriage is a new beginning irrespective of my background.
- I should find out my husband likes and dislikes. I should try to satisfy his needs.
- I should let my life and marriage be a beacon to advertise God.
- I should ensure my family's safety twenty-four-seven.
- I should prepare myself outwardly and inwardly for my husband.

To the Bride with Love

- I should learn whatever special skills that are needed for my husband's position so that I can give him adequate support.
- I should find my assignment in my marriage and fulfil it with God's help.
- I must learn to exercise self-control especially when I cannot have sexual intimacy with my husband.
- I should not forget to bless those whose lives have blessed me.
- I should show love and concern for my immediate and extended family.
- I should support my husband in prayers especially against evil associations.
- In overwhelming situations I must pray and fast seeking for God's direction and help.
- I should let my outward and inward presentation to my husband be one that will always win his approval even at critical times.
- I should prayerfully choose the right place, atmosphere and moment to talk to my husband on all matters and issues.
- I should appear before God, my maker in the attitude of reverence, praise, worship, adoration and humility.
- If I was given the chance to save my family or defend my race, I should use every opportunity to preserve, protect and promote the life of others especially the underprivileged and those of the household of faith.

THERE ON THE ROCK.

There is a place by ME
There on the rock
A place next to the Saviour
A place next to the Lord.

The place of comfort
There on the rock
Comfort from the devil
Comfort from the world.

The place of refuge
There on the rock
Refuge from sin and self
Refuge from sickness and Satan.

The place of refreshing
There on the rock
Refreshing from all life's fatigues
Refreshing from all life's failures.

The place of revelation
There on the rock
Revelation of God's glory
Revelation of God's mercy.

To the Bride with Love

The place of grace
There on the rock
Grace for you and I
Grace for all who would accept it.

The place of compassion
There on the rock
Compassion for the neglected
Compassion for the rejected.

The place of solitude
*There on the rock
God's still small voice to hear
God's abiding presence to feel.

© *Ola-Ojo. 16/1/96. *Exodus 33: 19 -20, Psalms 93: 22.*

Tambourine

Let your adornment be the inner self with the lasting beauty of a gentle and quiet spirit, which is very precious in God's sight.
1st Peter 3:4

Tambourine

As I am just blessing God for allowing a queen to visit me, there is another knock on the door. This time, it is a woman dressed like a princess. She greets me politely, gives me a tambourine as my wedding present and says she is grateful that I have allowed her in to share with me the joy of getting married. Who is this woman? I am thinking, as she begins to speak.

She extends a helping hand to the poor and opens her arms to the needy. She has no fear of winter for her household because all of them have warm clothes.
                                                Proverbs 31:20-21

The Bible warns that there will always be the poor in our midst. Daughter, be sensitive and observant, there will always be that person around you where you live or work or worship that is poor in what you are rich in. Please learn to open your hands to such a needy person. The fact that the person may not be in a position to pay you back makes your giving more significant to God. When we give to the poor, we are lending to the Lord and He pays a wonderful interest on this (Proverbs 19:17).

Prayerfully plan for your household in every thing including what they will wear. Be not concerned only with what you look like but be equally concerned about how your whole household is clothed. If you can afford it, save and prayerfully buy when there are sales. There are different seasons in the year, what is suitable for summer, if worn in autumn or winter will not only be unsuitable; it could be harmful to health.

Life is in seasons. Daughter, with God's help, prayerfully and adequately prepare ahead of each season. For yourself and your household. There will be the seasons of pregnancy, child bearing, weaning and toilet training for each of your children, requiring different forms of prayer and preparation. Setting up and maintaining an educational trust for each child going to primary school, secondary school, college/university is a good preparation towards the children's educational season for example.

Daughter------------- *(please insert your name here)* let me now share with you from my marital experiences.

No matter your background, never despise or belittle the things of God. I was a princess when my dad gave me away to the shepherd boy called David who later became the king. Though the beginning of your husband is small and insignificant, with his total obedience to God and your corporation, he will become who God ordained him to be. In your marriage, your primary responsibility is to protect and encourage your husband. Where he is weak, God has equipped you to be strong, so help him unreservedly. Protect him from 'killers' like food, friends, hobbies, dangerous family members, work mates, bosses, managers etc. Your husband's success or failure is yours as well. Your assignment as a wife also includes protecting your children and others in your household.

Daughter, don't be surprised if some of the people who initially supported your wedding turn and start to do things that can harm or destroy your marriage. One day my father, King Saul, for reasons best known to him sent for my husband to kill him. How my father who willingly gave me out in marriage, without being asked, could turn to kill my husband and make me a widow at an early age was most shocking to me. I had to protect my husband and so must you do too. I encouraged and made it possible for my husband to escape the king's wrath. Women generally, are more sensitive to feel and smell and they are usually able to perceive evil from afar. Use these God-given abilities in you to protect your husband and family from danger always. There are many out there who would like to have your husband as their dinner, child of God, please stand your ground, resisting the devil and his agents.

Many believe the Church is for the sick, needy, poor and homeless but they are not totally correct, as wise and successful people still seek Jesus. Your position should not deter you from being in the presence and house of the Lord. Rather, it should draw you there for in the presence of the Lord there is fullness of joy and at His right hand are pleasures forever more.

Tambourine

As my husband was bringing the Ark of the Covenant of God back home, I saw him dancing with young ladies to the extent that his clothes were almost falling off and I thought that would have been a great embarrassment to him and to me his wife. A man that brings embarrassment to himself, equally embarrasses his wife. Though I did not voice my comments out, I despised my husband in my heart. Little did I realise that heaven was recording my unspoken words. I got punished for that. Remember God heard Hannah's humanly unheard words and answered her prayers (1 Samuel 1:12, 19, 20).

What a terrible mistake I made, putting my husband's position above his relationship with God. It didn't matter after all if King David lost his robe and dignity before his maker that day and God blessed him for it.

I saw my husband the king dancing his heart out before the Lord but I was too proud to join in. All I was concerned about was that his royal robe was almost falling off. Daughter, please learn from me. Whenever you are in an environment of worship or in a position to worship the Lord with your dancing, singing, offering or service, you should jump at the opportunity because it is a privilege to be in such a position of potential blessing. You can use your energy positively rather than for criticising. How better it would have been if I had humbly danced to meet my husband and if possible given him a hand with his almost falling robe instead of watching from afar and boiling angrily within me.

Remember, that position, self esteem or status that makes you feel too big to openly praise Your maker from your inner most being was actually given to you by the Most High before whom there is none higher or more esteemed.

Many attend Church today but they aren't true worshippers of the Almighty God. With their mouth they sing praises but in their minds and hearts, they are far away from the Lord and the assembly of His people. May that not be your portion in Jesus' name.

One of the reasons why the work of the Lord is being delayed, I believe, is because of on-lookers and critics (as I was on that fateful day) in the house of the Lord. They take a conspicuous seat to watch, criticise, and condemn the move of the Holy Spirit and the work of the Church rather than becoming a part of the army of the Lord. Such people may come to Church on a daily basis but they stand condemned not justified and their prayer requests are rejected not honoured. Your attitude will ultimately determine your altitude in life.

My dear----------------------- *(please insert your name)* never despise your husband or God as both can lead to barrenness. If you find yourself being judgemental especially in Church during praise, worship, prayers, testimony, sermon or offering time, then focus on God and shut your eyes. Judging those who are sincerely serving the Lord in Church could be catastrophic. After the ceremony, I confronted King David about what I felt was embarrassing. He told me some home truths and I tell you, it affected our relationship afterwards. What is more, I couldn't retrieve my comments. A relationship that took many years to build can suddenly be destroyed with one wrong word. Wrong comments are like fresh eggs that once broken, leave bad smell and splash marks around for some time to come. Wrong words can also be likened to opening a can of worms that you're unable to control or contain.

Avoid being judgemental in your marriage for the same measure you use to judge will be used for you too. My husband dug out my family history in a way that was painful for me only after I had wrongly confronted him. Before coming to conclusions, find out all the facts, for things usually may not be as bad as you think if you do find out before passing your judgement. Ask for God's wisdom that will help you to build your home and relationship at all times.

I perceive the Shunnamite woman is eager to speak to you so I shall not delay both of you for much longer. Please before I take my leave, can we pray together?

> *Father, God of my husband King David, it is with assurance in You that I present your daughter ------------------- (insert your name here) before you this day in the name of Jesus. I thank you for bringing her to such an honourable and rewarding position of marriage. I humbly ask that You teach and train her so that she can protect her husband and family and that she might be able to stand her ground against every destroyer in Jesus' name. Please equip and help her in Jesus' name.*

Father in the name of Jesus, in this journey of marriage please help your daughter never to despise You or anything of Yours or her husband's. Help her never to scorn small beginnings. Help her especially in her thoughts that she will not give in to the devil rather, she will prayerfully guard her thoughts so that from her spirit may flow rivers of life, peace and joy. Grant her the grace not to accuse her husband falsely and help her not to be judgemental.

Jehovah, may the blood of Jesus that was shed on the cross of Calvary for our sins be sufficient to cleanse her from all iniquities such that she would not be barren in Jesus name we have prayed with thanksgiving.

Now I know why Princess Michal gave me this lovely tambourine you say to yourself. Then you begin to meditate on what you have learnt from her mainly that :
- I should give to the poor when and where I can.
- I should prayerfully plan for my household in everything including what they will wear.
- I should prayerfully prepare for every season of life.
- I must not despise small Godly beginnings.
- I should identify and stand my grounds against all forms of marriage destroyers.
- I must never be too big, rich etc. to praise God.
- I must support my husband in praising and serving God.
- I should avoid being judgemental and confrontational.
- I must never despise my husband or and God.

- I should participate in the work of the Lord and outreaches of the ministry avoiding becoming judgemental.
- I must be mindful and thoughtful of my words and what I say especially in my home.
- I should remember that my attitude will affect my ultimate altitude in life – marriage inclusive.

To the Bride with Love

MY PERSONAL NOTES

Beddings and Towels

Finally whatever is true, whatever is honourable, whatever is just, whatever is pure, whatever is pleasing, and whatever is commendable, if there is any excellence and if there is any praise, think about these things.
Philippians 4:8

To the Bride with Love

Beddings and Towels

My last guest was so brief yet her words were powerful enough, and I got thinking but then, I remembered she said the Shunnamite woman was on her way to see me. Then came the knock on the door and as I opened it, the Shunnamite woman came in beautifully and gorgeously dressed in royal purple. She brought for my wedding a colourful set of beddings and towels. We both sat down and she began to talk.

She quilts her own bedspreads. She dresses like royalty in gowns of finest cloth. Her husband is well known, for he sits in the council meeting with the other civic leaders.

Proverbs 31: 22 -23

The woman above pays attention to her appearance and comfort from the bedspread to what she wears. Your dressing as a woman especially says much about you and it is on that basis that many people will assess you, judge you, accept or reject you. There is indeed a *"demon of first impressions"* found literally everywhere. It was with great difficulty that King Saul allowed David to go to the battlefield for when they met, David was not dressed like a warrior but as a simple, perhaps poor, shepherd boy though he carried the anointing of the warrior. He had to write his own CV quickly in order to negate this demon of first impression *(see 1Samuel 17:17-50)*.

Before people can find out what stuff you are made of or what anointing you carry, it is not unusual for them to size you up according to your outward appearance. So learn to dress for where you are going in life, not where you are now or where you are coming from. A well-dressed woman is a blessing to and the glory of her husband. In some parts of the world, it is not uncommon for a husband to be assessed on the basis of what his wife wears. The lady described in the verse from Proverbs above is so well dressed that it influences the level of respect her husband commands among the civic leaders in her community.

A lady's dressing also usually affects her self esteem and how she carries herself in public. You will hardly find the daughter of any earthly king, who knows her right, dressing like a pauper. As the daughter of the Almighty King of Glory, apply the same principle to your dressing within and outside the home. May I stress that being well dressed doesn't mean dressing above your resources or income.It means you dress modestly and neatly within your income and budget. Please pay attention also to your body hygiene. Why should people know you are around by your bad smelling body odour? Why should people be afraid to talk to you because you have been fasting and that is your excuse for bad breath? Why should anyone be able to guess that you have just finished cooking when they meet you outside your home because it smells all over you?

Of equal importance is the state of the cleanliness and organisation of your home. Why should people know you are nursing a child because of the smell of the wee that meets them at the door or when they try to sit on the sofa in the living room? Why should the house be in a state of untidiness or disorder once you are married?

My dear ------------------, *(please insert your name)* that is my interpretation of that verse concerning the virtuous woman. Now, I am honoured to share a few useful marriage tips with you from my own marriage.

Indeed, I confirm that some staggering troubles may occur in marriage which money and position cannot solve. What then do you do to overcome such nagging, nerve wracking challenges? My husband and I were very wealthy but we had no child and that was very humbling. We tried all the doctors but we could still not achieve a pregnancy. We prayed a lot, but nothing worked. We finally got to the point of "let go and let God" do something about the issue as my husband and I felt that life must continue as normal with or without a child.

One day I observed a man visit our small community and I did not waste time in inviting him and his entourage home for a meal. Subsequently, I spoke to my husband and we made for him and his team today's equivalent of a "bed and meals" (not only breakfast). My dear, learn to carry your husband along in your hospitality - it pays. Be hospitable without necessarily looking for profit from the person you are helping. Even in your trouble, be observant and concerned about others and invest in them.

Learn to be contented and preserve yourself whatever your husband's condition is – medical, physical, financial, emotional or professional. My husband was old at the time I met the prophet and I could have engaged in some extra marital affairs but I kept myself. There will always be something that appears like a justifiable reason for having extra marital affairs today especially in the light of infertility but please shun every temptation. A fling today irrespective of the reason for it can open satanic doors into your life, marriage and home through deadly diseases – gonorrhoea, herpes, HIV/AIDS, emotional challenge – guilt, fear, spiritual or physical attacks and physical loss of life.

It was later that I realised that our guest was a man of God and one day he called me to ask what I would like him to do for me. *"Nothing"* was my reply. Unexpectedly, he said that I would have a baby! That came to pass later just as he had said. My dear, when a tested and proven to be true prophet gives a word from God, believe it and act on it (1John 4:4). Though my husband was already old, we exercised our faith in God and obeyed His servant in our matrimonial duties. God's word is never too late or too early to come to pass. Believe in God, then you will be established, believe in His prophets so shall you prosper (2 Chronicles 20:20).

Every good seed (investment) planted in rich and fertile soil always bears fruit. I took care of the man of God and God in turn took care of me using the same man of God, years later.

There will sometimes be emergencies in this journey you are about to take. First, in any emergency situation, much as you will be tempted, avoid panicking. Pray and avoid unnecessary delays as a few minutes could make the pendulum of any emergency swing from bad to worse. Our only son died one day on my lap after complaining of headaches. I laid his corpse on the prophet's bed and I sent to my husband for a donkey – the quickest means of transport then. I couldn't wait till my husband returned from the fields or go into a long discussion with him on what had happened. I briefly informed him of my decision to seek for help for our son.

In matters of life and death you may have to make decisions without the full knowledge of your husband. Be prayerful on how to act at such times. The only answer I could give to my husband's anxious inquiries as I set out for the prophet's place was, "It is well." Every mother ought to be careful with her confessions especially during times of crisis for 'What you call forth will come forth.' The devil sometimes sets people up to confess negatively about their situation especially when they are stressed. In emergencies, you can only use what you have stored. How much of God's word have you stored in your heart? Do you cash in on it in times of trouble?

I compromised on my comfort during the trip. It wasn't as important as getting our dead son back alive. You may temporarily have to sacrifice your comfort in emergency situations in order to get quick attention.

When I saw the prophet of God, I fell down before him in humility and told him our son was dead and I needed his help. I refused to return home without him and in the end, he came with me and God used him to bring our son back to life. I tell you, it pays to be humble and hospitable at all times.

Finally, when your problems overwhelm you, get people of like mind whom you can call on to spiritually bear you up in prayers and possibly attend to your physical needs. It doesn't matter what the physical, financial, material or emotional climate around you may be, hang in there, don't let go of God until He blesses you (Genesis 32:26-28). Some women have also received their loved ones from the dead through faith (Hebrews 11:35). I refused to let the man of God go until he returned home with me to attend to our dead son. God who did that for me many years ago is able to resurrect any dead issue in this marriage you are about to enter in Jesus' name.

I'm sure there is someone else on the way to see you but just before I go, can we just pray together please?

> *Almighty God, You who forgets no one, and who is able to bring life outside of nothing, please go before -------------------- (please insert your name) whom you created and is now going into this marriage. Father, please teach your daughter to be very prayerful, observant,*

kind and self-controlled. Lord, bless her enough to be in good position to meet other people's needs. Help her Lord in any emergency situation that might come her way, to confess Your Word and at such times, please send her Your own prophet through whom her desired miracle will come to pass in Jesus' name. Father we forbid every form of infertility or dryness, be it physical, financial, social, emotional or spiritual, that might want to attack this new home in Jesus' name. We pronounce Your blessing according to Genesis 1: 26 to the end and we command Your fruitfulness on all sides for them in Jesus' name. Lord, in agreement we forbid any and every form of illness or disease that might want to shorten the life of any of her children in Jesus name. Thank You everlasting Father for in Jesus' name we have prayed with thanksgiving. Amen.

She left you some minutes ago but her words keep echoing in your mind and this is what you remember from her talk:

- I should pay attention to every aspect of my appearance and that of my household.
- I should be aware of the demon of first impression so learn to dress well always.
- I should pay particular attention to my body hygiene; avoiding bad breath, bad body odour, smelly dress etc.
- I should dress for where I am going not where I am now.
- I should be aware that my dressing would affect my self-esteem.

- Being well dressed is a blessing to and the glory of my husband.
- I should learn to let go of every overwhelming challenge and let God into it.
- I should be observant in spite of my own challenges, try and meet other people's needs within my income.
- I should carry my husband along in my hospitality and generosity.
- I should be contented in my marriage in spite of any obvious yet unmet needs.
- There is no excuse for me having extra marital affairs even with any 'man of God'.
- God's words and promises will always come to pass.
- I must believe in God and in His prophets.
- I should prayerfully and tactically handle emergencies.
- I may have to ignore my comfort in times of emergencies.
- In critical conditions, any delay can decide life or death.
- I must always remember that what I call forth will come forth.
- I can only call forth what is in my heart so I should learn to store God's words in my heart.
- I should have prayer partners that can comfort and intercede for and with me.
- I should approach God and His representative in humility, adoration and praise.
- I need to learn to tarry in the presence of God and His proven prophet so that I can have my needs met and my prayers answered.

- I must remember that God is able to bring back to life any dead thing that is precious to me.

CAFETERIA

Cafeterias provide food.
Various dishes for various times
Some are spicy; others are not
Some are sweet, others are sour
Cold and hot drinks, snacks, sweets and fruits.

Some dishes take long to prepare and cook
Others a few minutes or perhaps seconds
Some dishes look really attractive and tempting
Other dishes simply look very plain and uninviting.

Some dishes are made for certain groups of people:
Vegetarians who don't eat any animal product,
The diabetic or some others on special diets,
And many little children love sweet meals most.

Some dishes may not taste very nice but we eat them
To make us grow healthy and strong
Such are the lessons on faith, love and hope
Reflecting these in our lives makes us Christlike and useful.

To the Bride with Love

Human beings have the tendency to be hungry for food.
As well as thirsty for a drink, cold or hot.
While some live to eat most of their lives
Others eat to live and face life's challenges.

At meal times the cafeteria trolleys are fully stocked
Some cafeterias have complete self-service
In others, orders are placed with the stewards.
In school cafeterias, there is minimal choice.

Stewards sometimes stand at the back of food trolleys
Watching customers and refilling the food trolleys,
Giving a helping hand in serving customers,
With someone at the cash till to be paid for the food taken.

The Bible is God's cafeteria for the world
With enough food for the hungry and drink for the thirsty
Every human spiritual need is already catered for,
Meeting every age group, ability and need.

The word of God is there at all times, in all seasons
The Psalms for encouragement, Proverbs for wisdom
Genesis for the creation story and revelations for the latter days
Matthew, Mark, Luke and John for Jesus' ministry
Ephesians, Corinthians, Colossians, Galatians
For rebuke and encouragement.

To the Bride with Love

What then are you having, friend, at the next meal time?
In the earthly cafeteria, we pay for our choice,
In the Bible, God's cafeteria to mankind, Christ has paid
In full by His death on the cross
And by His stripes we are healed.

Heavenly hosts watch what we do at meal times
Christ on God's right hand, always interceding on our behalf
Angels waiting upon us for our orders in God
How often do you visit God's cafeteria for mankind?

Jeremiah 31:25. © O.Ola- Ojo 20/04/96

To the Bride with Love

MY PERSONAL NOTES

Bottle of Olive Oil

Let us hold fast to the confession of our hope without wavering for He who has promised is faithful.
Hebrews 10:23

To the Bride with Love

Bottle of Olive Oil

There's a soft knock on my door. I open it excitedly and my next guest comes in with a small bottle of olive oil in her hand. To me she appears to be rich but I am thinking, *"What is she doing with the bottle in her hand?"* She greets me and gives me the bottle of olive oil as she sits down.

She makes belted linen garments and sashes to sell to the merchants. She is clothed with strength and dignity, and she laughs with no fear of the future...
Proverbs 31:24-25

The woman above is in the garment industry - making and selling them to merchants. She is a very busy person and is clothed with strength, respect, distinction and majesty. My dear, what is in your hand that you can use on an industrial or enterpreneurial level and become a merchant as well? What services can you provide on a commercial scale or what can you do that will bring out the creativity in you? Please think of how you can turn your hobby into a cash machine.

The virtuous wife above laughs and has no fear of the future, for her entire household is well protected spiritually, financially and physically. For instance, being a woman doesn't prevent you from taking out a robust comprehensive insurance for yourself and your household. That way, in today's terms, you can laugh at the future. Your gender as a woman ought not to deter you from any profession or stop you from reaching the top of your chosen profession. In the same way nothing should stop you from trading in shares on the stock market or in engaging in the property or information technology business. Essentially, what you need is to gain sufficient knowledge of these investment ideas and appropriately research them to know when it is best to embark on any of them because of the risks involved.

My dear ---------------------- *(please insert your name)*, I consider myself privileged to be among those chosen to speak to you today. Please pardon me, as I feel led to speak to you on an area that is mentioned in most marriage vows but hardly discussed before the wedding. Long may the Lord make your marriage to last in Jesus' name. Amen.

Can you remember for how long you both were in this relationship before you decided to get married? Can you identify some learning you have had or are having before this marriage? While many couples to be have received some form of premarital counselling, hardly any are prepared for separation or death after marriage.

First, my dear, know that good things happen to bad people and bad things too do happen to good people. All the same, it is better to be good all the time. Just as there are seasons of autumn, winter, spring and summer so there are seasons of life characterised by trials and tribulations, peace and tranquillity, good times and bad times. Remember too, that whatever the season you experience in this forth-coming marriage, seasons are 'seasonal' - they come and go.

That you and I serve God will not prevent us from encountering some natural attacks like sickness and death. My husband was a faithful, caring, God-seeking, loving husband and father to our two boys, but he took ill and died after a while. I was very devastated to lose a good friend, companion, husband and breadwinner. Then came the creditor's harassment and threat to take our two sons away. I found myself in a terrible mess. In our days, there were no insurance policies, let alone life assurance to fall back on when my husband died. Now that such things are available, I strongly suggest that you and your husband invest in a robust life assurance that can take care of you or your husband and the children should one of you go home earlier than envisaged

Rarely does anyone prepare for the death call of his or her spouse but it is a sure event that must happen: often with no prior warning. Should your husband die before you, after the period of mourning, please pick up yourself and go on with life. 'How would I do that', you ask? Where would I start? How could I go on without someone to support me? Who could love me as my husband would? Please do seek for counselling and prayers, as no generalised answer may be good enough or appropriate for your own situation.

Secondly, the solution to your marital problem is in your house, if only you look for it and take wise counsel. However, be careful where you take counsel and from whom. Believe in God and in His proven prophets. Little as your *"except"* may be (e.g. writing, speaking, sewing, baking, cooking, typing, professional, management skills etc.), when given to Master Jesus, He will bless and use it for your lifetime financial, spiritual and material release. Give your *"except"* to the Lord and watch Him multiply and bless it. God created each of us with gifts, some of which you may not be aware you possess.

Thirdly, the devil may want to take your children away from you, but resist him in the name of Jesus. Today's *"creditors"* include mortgage or rent payments that keep you working away from home and being with your children less often than you would have wanted to. The *"creditor"* could also be that thing that lures your children away from the Lord, activities that if pursued could shorten their life span e.g. the occult, drug addiction, drinking, sexual indulgence outside of marriage (fornication) etc. In addition to your training your children, please involve them in seeking God's face regularly, particularly when a problem needs to be solved. Don't underestimate the effect of your children witnessing God's rescue or supernatural provision in times of need.

Be interested in your neighbours and be kind to them because you might be the only Christian they get to see or know. You might one day need them or they may find you approachable. Also, be careful of your confession at all times and in all situations, for your words can either create or destroy. If you must talk, then speak positively. Let your speech be in line with God's Word and teach your children to do the same. The power of life and death is in the tongue, please be very careful how you use it.

Always give feedback to those who help you, since this will encourage them to help you as well as others in future. Some miracles are completed instantaneously, while others are in stages. Giving an update or a feedback to the person God uses to provide a solution to your problem also gives you the opportunity of receiving further instructions from them, should your miracle be that which occurs progressively.

Finally, I mustn't leave without letting you know that you can be successful enough as a businessperson to meet all your present and future needs without sleeping around or compromising on your faith or Godly values.

Like my other sisters who have shared with you already have done, shall we pray please?

> *Loving Father,*
> *Thank You for the opportunity of sharing some of my marital experiences with -------------------- (please insert your name). Lord, please grant that she and her husband will have a happy marriage and may none of them die young in Jesus' name. Grant your daughter the anointing to bring up the children you will give to them in the fear of the Lord.*

Lord in Jesus name, grant Your daughter the wisdom and ability to deal with any creditor who might want to forcefully take away her children into any form of slavery.

Lord, as your daughter looks into her life and home, please open her eyes to recognize what you have placed in her hands both to meet her immediate needs and to launch her family into a better and secured future in Jesus' name we have prayed. Amen

You return to your seat with the bottle of pure olive oil in your hand and you are still captivated by what lessons you gained from the Widow's visit:

- I must find something that I can do on an entrepreneurial level.
- I should find and use the creativity in me.
- Bad things do happen to good people.
- I must remember that life is in seasons and seasons are phasal.
- Serving God does not immune one from natural or spiritual attacks.
- I must be careful where and whose counsel I receive should I need it.
- I should be aware of today's creditors such as the mortgage lender.
- I should be aware that the devil would always want to take my children.

- I must have a life insurance policy for my husband and myself.
- Having an investment or insurance for each child is profitable.
- I should realise that the solution to all of our marital challenges is already within me.
- I must protect my children from the creditors of life.
- I should be kind to and interested in my neighbours.
- I must watch and ensure that my confessions are in line with the word of God.
- I should learn to update those who God uses in my life.
- I can be a successful businesswoman from within the confines of my home.

Useful books to read:
1. **Rich Woman** by Kim Kiyosaki published by RICH Press. ISBN 1-933914-00-9.
2. **The Mocha Manual** to turing your passion into profit, by Kimberly Seals-Allers published by Amistad. ISBN 978-1-6075-377-3.

Bag of Grains

In the morning sow your seed, and at evening do not let your hands be idle: for you do not know which will prosper, this or that, or whether both alike will be good.
Ecclesiastes 11:6

Bag of Grains

Opening the door for the next person knocking, I see a middle aged woman holding some grains in a bag. She looks different from the other women who have stopped by and again, I ask myself, "Who is this woman"? She greets me and hands me the bag of grains in her hand, and then we both take our seats.

When she speaks, her words are wise, and kindness is the rule when she gives instructions. She carefully watches all that goes on in her household and does not have to bear the consequences of laziness.

Proverbs 31:26-27

The virtuous wife makes it a point to speak when necessary. She freely expresses herself, but in a wise manner. Her words are not only wise but also kind especially when she gives instructions. Proverbs 14:1 says a wise woman builds her home but the foolish tears hers down.

My sister ---------------------- *(please insert your name here)*, the Book of Proverbs also says that the words of the wise are soothing enough to bring healing to the bones.

There is so much wrong in the world today perhaps because many women who are in position to speak out are not doing so. And if they are, maybe they are saying the wrong things to their children, brothers, uncles, husbands and others that are in a position to help change the world into a better place for all to live in.

If the Lord gives you a voice in your marriage, then by all means sister, please speak out for God and the good of humanity. What comes out of your mouth is not only a reflection of what is in your heart; it is also what makes you who you are. A wise person once said 'show me your actions and I will tell you your thoughts'. When you speak, what usually comes out - curses or blessing? Words of wisdom or foolishness? Words are so important that God created the world with them and has maintained the world by the same words ever since. For every miracle of Jesus, He spoke sometimes to the problem or to the person involved or to those who brought the person needing the miracle. Words are so powerful that God doesn't do anything without speaking first. Wise words bring life, encouragement, motivation, and freedom. Please learn to use wise words in your home and always ensure that your motive for speaking is right.

Learn to give instructions to members of your household and those who will work with you. Be watchful over all that goes on in your household. Avoid laziness, as it has many terrible spiritual and physical consequences. The book of Proverbs says a lazy person refuses to go out, claiming that a lion is waiting in the streets to kill him or her but that such a person will soon face hunger and poverty (Proverbs 26:13). There's no excuse for laziness. Mothers that are lazy in prayers hardly hear from God concerning their families and may not be sensitive to praying at the appropriate time and for the vital needs of their household. Also, failure to root your children in prayers leaves them like a reed that is vulnerable to negative and sometimes destructive winds of life.

Many who are lazy in disciplining their children from an early age end up bearing the consequences of waywardness, selfishness, self-centeredness and all the vices of the enemy. Those who are lazy in training their children on how to handle money and wealth will have to deal with issues of untold debts, joblessness, and loss of property, bankruptcy, armed robbery and cultism in their children who engage in these vices in order to maintain a wealthy lifestyle.

My dear --------------------*(please insert your name)* let me now talk to you on the issues of marriage from my own personal experience. I was a foreigner from Moab with no hope, no husband, brother or father-in-law: no one but God - I mean the Almighty God under whose wing I sought for refuge; the One who gave me hope; the fruit of the womb; and a reason to smile again! Through my relationship with my in-laws, I became an heir to the Commonwealth of God.

First, if you choose to marry a foreigner, be much aware that there will be a cultural change both ways. A wise person once said "it takes a little while to understand a language, but it sometimes takes a life time to understand a culture." Be aware that there may be a huge gap between what is acceptable in your culture and what is not in your husband's culture. Take time to learn your husband's traditional dishes, salutations, outfits, what things and dates are peculiar to him and so on. In other words, be prepared for some cultural changes in addition to the individual changes every married person goes through.

How you perceive and treat your in-laws will strengthen or weaken your marriage and relationship with them. If you see them as a blessing not a curse, and therefore treat them with love and respect, then you are likely to gain their support and trust. When my husband died, the existing bond between my mother in-law and I was strengthened so much that I volunteered to go with her to Bethlehem to begin life again. Mothers in-law should not be seen as threats but as blessings as there is so much that you can learn from them when the relationship is cordial.

Secondly you are married to a family not only to your husband so be careful and prayerful about how you deal with your in-laws. Though my husband, his brother and their father had died unexpectedly, I felt that I was still part of the family and couldn't afford to leave my old mother in-law alone by herself. Learn to identify with, and share in the joy, hard times and sorrows of your in-laws.

Orpah, my late brother in-law's wife also decided to follow Naomi (our mother in-law) and the three of us left together for Bethlehem but Orpah later turned back to Moab while I continued the journey with my mother in-law. For me, it was a great responsibility and also a privilege to look after my mother-in-law, for she had always been a blessing not a curse. My dear lady, in what ways have you been or will you be a blessing to your future in-laws? When last did you call, visit or pray for them? When last did you bless them by giving appropriate gifts and seeking after their welfare?

Thirdly, your input in your marriage will be noted not only where you are now, but worldwide. You cannot hide from God and His purpose for your life. You also cannot hide from people especially those you have no idea are watching you. In Bethlehem, my going to work to bring food for myself and my mother in-law was noticed and rewarded although my aim was not for personal gain but to keep both of us alive until we could sort out ourselves.

Fourthly, I learnt that serving your in-laws could lead to eternal blessing. My mother in-law taught me how to get a husband again and she supported me all the way without an atom of jealousy or ill will. God, through her, gave me the best husband by the name of Boaz, my father in-law's kinsman who redeemed me from shame, poverty, insecurity and homelessness, physical and sexual cold. What more, I conceived and gave birth to Obed the father of Jesse, the father of David, the father of Jesus Christ – the world's saviour and redeemer! I who came from a cursed background was now accepted into the commonwealth of God and specially blessed to be in the lineage of Jesus Christ.

God is able to replace whatever the enemy steals from you.

I thought I had lost the most important part of my life when my first husband died; little did I realise that God was preparing me for a restoration much more than I could ever have imagined.

Finally, daughter, when confronted with tough issues of life, it is only under the wings of the Most High God that one can find shelter, protection, comfort, victory and direction. Under His Wings, all curses are neutralized and one finds eternal blessings and joy. Run to God just as you are. He is willing to bless you and keep you safe in the hollow of His hands. Whatever adversity God permits in your life is not sent to destroy but to cleanse and develop you.

Shall we pray before I take my leave?

> *Loving Father,*
> *Thank You for the opportunity of sharing some of my marital experiences with --------------------- (please insert your name). Lord as she goes into this marriage, please grant her Your divine favour and that of her in-laws that they may be able to dwell in peace in Jesus' name. Father, grant Your daughter the strength and resources to support her immediate and extended family including her in-laws in Jesus' name. May she find shelter, protection, comfort, victory and direction under Your wings as the Most High God in Jesus' name we pray with thanksgiving. Amen*

What an exposition on relationships with in-laws, a much-dreaded topic among young people today. I just cannot thank Ruth enough for dealing with the subject of in-laws especially from her robust experience. I learnt from her that:

- I should apply wisdom in my speech to others
- Watch over my thoughts as that will reflect in my speech and affect my life.
- I should speak for others if and when I have the opportunity.
- I must be aware and mindful of all that goes on in my home and marriage.
- I should avoid every form of laziness in my marriage and home.
- Should I marry from another culture I should be aware of the possibility of cultural differences, and therefore I should be open to learning, be understanding and be tolerant.
- I should be in good terms with my in-laws.
- I should be part of my husband's family from the time I say 'I do".
- My input – positive or negatively in the marriage will be obvious to all to see.
- I should learn to joyfully and purposely serve my in-laws (so long as it is within my ability to do so).
- Serving my in-laws can bring eternal blessing.
- God is able to restore whatever I lose in my marriage.
- It is only under the wings of the Almighty God that I can find secured shelter and comfort.

Most of this chapter has been taken from 'Refuge Under His

Wings' by Oluwakemi O. Ola-Ojo published by Protokos Publishers. ISBN: 978-0-9557898-0-9.

GOD HAS ANOTHER PLAN

When you lose your beloved one to sickness
Despite the best available medical care
And the loss is too much to bear
Be assured beloved, for God has another plan.

When the illness seems to be tarring for so long
And doctors have run short of medications to use
And the pains are becoming very much unbearable
Hang in there beloved, for God has another plan.

When you suddenly lose your precious job
And the bills are rolling in, in the usual envelopes
With no new job in sight at the least
Don't give up beloved, for God has another plan.

When the creditors are on you back or at your tail
And you have not been able to meet your financial obligations
Due to no known fault of yours
Don't commit suicide beloved, for God has another plan.

When you fail that professional examination yet again
Despite your burning the midnight oil and working hard
With no courage to read let alone face another examination
Don't give up beloved, for God has another plan.

Bag of Grains

When your trusted spouse or business partner walks out on you
At the most 'inappropriate time' and in an unpleasant manner
Children to look after or business deals to sort out all by yourself
Don't doubt in yourself, for God has another plan.

When you fail to be given that much wanted business contract
Despite you wonderful briefs and excellent presentations
And the many hours and resources you have committed to it
Never give up beloved, for God has another plan.

God's plans are not close to any plans of ours
HIS plans for each one of us who are His children
Are plans of good not of evil to cause us any harm
*To give us a future and bring us to an expected end.

His plans are by far different from our plans
In the same manner as His ways are far from ours:
Like the sun, moon and stars are far from us,
His thoughts are farther and beyond our imagination.

In that present circumstance dearly beloved,
God through Jesus Christ is waiting for you
Give all your loss and failed plans to the Lord
And watch Him unfold His wonderful plan for you.

© O. Ola-Ojo. 22.10.02 *Jeremiah 29:11.

To the Bride with Love

MY PERSONAL NOTES

The Bible and Devotional Book

Do your best to present yourself to God as one approved by Him, a worker who has no need to be ashamed, rightly explaining the word of truth.
2Timothy 2:15

To the Bride with Love

The Bible and Devotional Book

My last guest for the day comes in dressed as a builder but holding in her hands as well, a Bible and some leaflets. I just can't figure out who she might be. She nicely and calmly greets and introduces herself: *"I am Priscilla, the wife of Acquilla."* She then gives me a Bible and some tracts and a Bible study guide. As we both take our seats, I realize that even though I have listened to nine women already, I'm still excited and very eager to hear what she has to tell me.

Her children stand and bless her. Her husband praises her: "There are many virtuous and capable women in the world, but you surpass them all!" Charm is deceptive, and beauty does not last; but a woman who fears the Lord will be greatly praised. Reward her for all she has done. Let her deeds publicly declare her praise.
                                                Proverbs 31:28-31

Should anyone ask your family members now to say something about you what are they likely to say? Curse, swear or bless? Whether you and I like it or not, there will come a point in our life when your immediate family –children, husband will talk about you. Will they stand up to celebrate your life or not? It is only in fearing the Lord, displaying love and working diligently that true praises can be sang.

I am most grateful to God for allowing me to encourage you in the new journey you are about to undertake. For you as a Christian trusting God, this journey will be for as long as you both shall be alive. My predecessors have spoken from their wealth of experiences and the Bible. I'm sure that you have learnt a lot from them. Now, I will very briefly share a few marriage tips with you from my story.

First, learn to support your husband's trade not only on your knees praying but also in your action and deeds. Be genuinely interested in his vocation. My husband and I were both tent makers so we worked together. If you're fortunate and can by mutual understanding work in the same house or office with your husband, why not try it out?

Secondly, learn to open your house and use your assets to support ministers or ministries in whatever capacity that God has empowered you. Hospitality always pays in the end so do yourself a favour by being warm to those who stop by your abode. From the accounts in the Bible and my personal experience, I can confidently say it pays to be generous especially to strangers and those who may never be able to return your generosity. This is because you never can tell when you will be hosting another Apostle Paul that notable man of God or Elisha the great prophet.

You can support the spread of the gospel by opening up your home for Bible study or other Christian groups. How about having the youths in your community taught and mentored in a youth club that you are part of even if not in your home?

You need to be ahead of the devil and his cohorts. "How?" I know you want to ask and I will tell you. It is very simple. Read the Bible yourself and know it personally, for in it is the wisdom of God to build your home and family. Be in tune with God in prayers as you discuss with Him every issue of life and hear Him talk back to you.

Finally, learn to motivate yourself, and then it will be easier to motivate others around you. Don't be afraid to correct others in love. When you need to correct others young or old, be discrete about it and don't do it publicly. We once had a guest who was preaching about Jesus but he was unaware that Jesus had died and risen from the dead by then. I took this man aside and told him so. He was glad and so was I.

Sister, I wish you all the very best of God's blessings in your forthcoming marriage. Please let us pray before I go:

> *Father, in the name of Jesus, I bring Your daughter -------------- (please insert your name) before You with a heart of gratitude. Thank You for giving her a wonderful and God-loving husband. Together may You equip them in their chosen, God-ordained vocational services in Jesus name. Teach and help Your daughter to make her home open to those who need fellowship, those who*

need an expression of Your love, and those who need food, drink or shelter and warmth. In Your mercy, bless the works of her hands and help her to be a very supportive wife, to the vocation and ministry that You have given to her husband in Jesus' name we pray with thanksgiving. Amen.

Short, brief but rich was her talk and like my other guests I began to ponder on what I learnt from her:

- I should be aware that my married life will be assessed by many. I dare not misrepresent God.
- I should support my husband in prayers and by my positive actions.
- If I can, work with or around my husband's job.
- I should open my home to the work of the ministry and support ministers.
- I should learn to correct others discretely.
- I should learn to motivate myself and others around me.

'What love! What a unique privilege to have had these ten women of virtue stop by to wish me well before my marriage', you say to yourself. As you glance at the various symbolic yet significant gifts that each one of them brought for you, you immediately remember the advice from each of them. Falling on your knees in prayers, you raise your hands to heaven thanking God for such an opportunity and trusting Him for a successful marriage ahead of you. You feel more equipped and determined to say 'I do' to the love of your life, knowing that God will help you all the way.

OPPORTUNITY TO BECOME A CHRISTIAN

Dear Father in heaven,
Thank you for the privilege of reading this book. 'Indeed I have sinned and come short of Your glory.' I am grateful to You for sending Jesus Christ into this world to come to die on the cross of Calvary for me. I believe in my heart that Jesus Christ paid for my sins, past, present and future. I believe Jesus Christ was buried and on the third day He rose from the dead. I believe that Jesus Christ will come back again. I confess with my mouth and I accept Him now to be my Lord.
Master, Saviour, Brother, and Friend. I ask in Your mercy for the infilling of theHoly Spirit so that with His help, I can live a victorious life becoming all that You have ordained me to be in Jesus' name I pray with thanksgiving. Amen.

If after reading this book you said the above prayer and became born-again, 'Congratulations! You are Born Again' is a booklet for those who have done so through reading this book. It is a free booklet that we would like you to have. In it, the frequently asked questions are answered and this will get you on the way to growing in your newfound faith in God. You can download this free booklet from our website: www.protokospublishers.com

You may also contact any of the organisations listed at the end of the book.

I look forward to hearing from you soon.
O. Ola–Ojo

OTHER BOOKS BY THE AUTHOR:

Provocation, Prayer and Praise
(December 2004 & 2009)

Complimentary to The Christian and Infertility this book focuses on the story of an infertile woman in the Bible, her provocations, prayer and praise. Whatever makes you incomplete, unfulfilled, less than whom God made you to be, whatever issue of life that the enemy uses to provoke you calls for prayer.

Key features include:
- Some known medical reasons for infertility in the women.
- Why Hannah went to the house of God in spite of her barrenness.
- Is it true that the husband is much more than 10 sons to the infertile woman?
- When, where and how to address the source/cause of your provocation.
- God's part and your part in that promise.
- God is able to met that humanly impossible need of yours.
- A time to celebrate and praise God.

Book Details:
Paperback: 128 pages
Language English
ISBN-13: 978-0-9557898-3-0

A Reader from London, 7 Jan 2006 on Amazon.co.uk
An excellent easy to read and understand book. The principles shared in this book though primarily are for those trying for a baby could as well be applied to any area of hurt and un-fulfilment.

 :www.protokospublishers.com

To the Bride with Love

The Christian and Infertility
(December 2004 & 2009)

The Christian and Infertility addresses one of the often neglected needs of Christian couples. It gives an insight into infertility from the biblical and medical perspectives. It is written not only for potential fruitful couples but for pastors, family and friends of these couples. It is written that the Body of Christ might be fully equipped to know and support couples who are facing the challenge of infertility at present.

Key features include:
- Childleness in the Bible and lessons to learn;
- Some possible physical, medical and environmental causes of infertility;
- Some known spiritual causes of infertility;
- The man and low sperm count;
- Some of the available treatment optons in the UK;
- Choice of fertility treatment;
- Should a christian professional be involved in fertility treatment?

Book Details:
Paperback: 146 pages
Language English
ISBN-13: 978-0-9557898-2-3

*A reviewer from Glen Burnie, USA, 29 Oct 2007 on Amazon.co.uk'
The book is a great eye-opener for all. It sheds light on infertility from the medical and spiritual angle. This gives the reader a balance because i believe every human being is made up of both physical and spiritual part. To get a balance in life, the two parts must be well fed. One must not concentrate on the spiritual and neglect the physical part. The book also reminds us that God has a way of sorting us out.... The book is quite inspiring. I will recommend this book to everybody trusting God for any form of blessing from God to go get one and apply it to his or her situation. It will definitely bless you and yours'.*

 :www.protokospublishers.com

Obstetrics and Gynaecology Ultrasound - A Self-Assessment Guide

June 2005 Churchill Elsevier Publishers, UK.

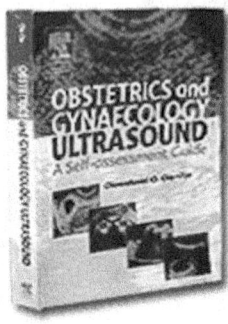

This self-assessment guide is a structured questions and answer book that develops the reader's understanding capability using a simple method in treating related topics. Clinical indications are presented with their corresponding ultrasound findings using appropriate illustrations. A case study approach is followed; presenting the clinical and ethical dilemmas that might arise while encouraging students to think. The aim is to reinforce theoretical knowledge within a clinical environment.

Key features:
- Over 600 high-resolution ultrasound images
- Cover a wide spectrum of ultrasound curriculum.
- Includes a detailed study of fertility.
- Aids quick understanding of subject matter.
- 468 pages.

ISBN-10: 0443064628
ISBN-13: 978-0443064623
Book Dimensions: 24 x 16.8 x 2.6 cm

"...This excellent new book is a study guide... This is an attractive paperback that should be essential reading for trainee obstetric and gynaecological sonographers, whether they are radiographers or radiology or obstetric trainees. It will be of particular value to those preparing for the RCOG/RCR Diploma in Advanced Obstetric Ultrasound and to specialist registrars in obstetrics and gynaecology undertaking special skills modules in fetal medicine, gynaecological ultrasound and infertility..."

The Obstetrician & Gynaecologist, www.rcog.org.uk/togonline
Book reviews 2006

Reviewer Ann Harper MD FRCPI FRCOG.
Consultant Obstetrician and Gynaecologist
Royal Jubilee Maternity Service, Belfast., UK

 :www.protokospublishers.com

GOOD MUMS, BAD MUMS
(June 2005 & 2009)

This is in two parts, the main chapter that can be used for personal or group study, and an accompanying exercise section. The privileged position of a mother is in her being a co-creator with God and bringing forth life (lives). This book compliments one of God's previous revelations to me as contained in the book titled Good Dads, Bad Dads'. While the father could be likened to the pilot of the family plane, the mother can be likened to the force behind the plane – positive or negative. Good mothers are not only co-creators with God, they also do nurture as well as nourish their children physically, emotionally and spiritually.

Keys Features:
- Were all the mothers in the Bible god mothers?
- Lessons from the strengths and weakness of seven mothers.
- Be encouraged - you are not alone in the assignment of motherhood.
- Be motivated in the areas of your strengths.
- Learn ways of supporting your husband and children.

Book Details:
Paperback: 162 pages
Language English
ISBN-13: 978-0-9557898-1-6
Book Dimensions: 21.4 x 14 x 1.4 cm

I appreciate the author's method of writing. It is always exciting holding her book to read. Personally, 'Good Mums, Bad Mums' has been a blessing to me in no small measure. The book is rich, it is loaded with physical and spiritual uplifting subjects. To all existing and potential mothers, this book is a MUST read. At the end of every chapter there is an exercise to do that will help in re-examining your life spiritually and in other ways. I encourage all women to get and use this book as a guide in raising their children. You will be glad you did.

Pastor Mrs T Adegoke
Freedom Arena
London, UK

 :www.protokospublishers.com

To the Bride with Love
(2007 & 2010)

Every wise woman preparing to get married knows she will need sound advice, practical tips and solid, heartfelt prayers, of those who have travelled on the road she is about to journey on. In this book, ten women of different age groups, from different backgrounds and cultures who wedded under various circumstances, individually share their experience with the bride in an intimate, very candid and unforgettable way.

Book details:
Paperback: 134 pages
Language English
ISBN-13: 978-0-9557898-4-7
ISBN:978-1-4343-0252-6(sc)

Book Dimensions: 22.4 x 15 x 1 cm

To the Bride with Love is the perfect bride's evergreen companion. The content is suitable, relevant and applicable even decades after the wedding day.
To the Bride with Love is an ideal wedding gift on its own. It can also accompany any other gift (big or small) that you have for the bride but take this hint... the bride will keep thanking you for the book years and years after.

'One of the best', 19 Jul 2008 on Amazon.com
Sade Olaoye "clare4good" (United Kingdom)
This book has really helped my marriage from the onset as I got it as a wedding gift, God bless the giver. It's a must read for relationship improvement and God's guidance. I recommend people to get for oneself and also as a great blessing for someone else in love. "To the Bride with Love"

Review by Oyinlola Odunlami CEO.
Shallom Bookshop, London UK

The writing style of Oluwakemi is unique, peculiar and distinct to herself. I recommend To the Bride with Love to wives, wives to be, mothers, mentors, youth leaders and workers. Why? The clarity, the focus and the intent of this book is so empowering, encouraging and enlightening that it will definitely mould or re mould a life to achieve its purpose. The truth is, there are very few books that have depth as well as help you to achieve your goals and arrive at your destination. Many books tend to excite you but have no depth; you read and you forget; they do not really change you but this book, To the Bride with Love will definitely leave a word in your spirit and move you to your next level!

I believe that this is also a book that pastors will find useful as a manual for marriage counselling, because many books on marriage focus mostly on what you as an individual can gain, your own personal satisfaction while little is said about the sacrifices involved and their importance. As my pastor usually says, it is important to learn from those who have gone ahead, understand why some were successful and others weren't, so that we won't fall where they fell, rather, we would gain more speed, achieve our goals and thereby glorify Christ.

So, I invite you not only to get a copy of this life-changing manual for yourself, but also to put it into as many hands as you can afford to, for then the world will definitely benefit and your life will be a blessing to many.

 :www.protokospublishers.com

Refuge Under His Wings

"an exhaustive analysis of the Book of Ruth in the Bible. The author combines her deep Christian conviction and excellent knowledge of the Holy Scriptures to produce a must read for every Christian, married or single. The book is interspaced with beautifully written prayers, which enables the reader to pause, pray and meditate on the revelations received... The book is also loaded with poetry like 'Thy will be done oh Lord' for those who may be facing an uncertain future or on a cross road of decisions."

Dr E B Ekpo MD, FRCP
Queen Elizabeth Hospital, Christian Fellowship,
Woolwich, London. UK

"...[a] ...spiritually sound book... a fine work of thoughtful reading and study... I therefore recommend it to every Christian, married or single....
Pat Roach Senior Pastor
New Covenant Church.
Wandsworth Branch, London. UK.

Book details:
Paperback: 100 pages
Language English
ISBN-10: 095578980X
ISBN-13: 978-0955789809

This book feeds the soul. Most of all I loved the poetry. It gives you time to savour the thoughts as reader. There is a good mix of poetry and prose. To look at the story of Ruth in depth gave good spiritual food. You can pause and take it in at your own pace. The meditation on Psalm 121 was good also. There's nothing like reading a Psalm slowly and meditating on its contents. The author's own reflections allow you to see the book through someone else's eyes. A good read.

Book Review: by **Gaby Richards**, London, UK.

 :www.protokospublishers.com

Grace or Works?
(2010)

This book makes you examine a lot of issues in your life, family relationships in particular, that you may have taken for granted or totally ignored. As conveyed right from the rhetorical question posed in the title, Grace or Works?, the author stirs you towards asking yourself pertinent questions, thinking through for answers and even getting solutions for unresolved problems.

Have you heard of prodigal wives, husbands, mothers or prodigal fathers? This book identifies and defines them clearly. For anyone experiencing a crises in their relationship with such prodigal family members, this book, which is based on the parable of the "Prodigal son" in Luke 15:11-32 is a one-stop resource material to meet your counselling needs. And just in case you happen to be the prodigal who has caused your relatives much sorrow, there is hope for you in this book.

Interspersed with prayers for you by the author and specific prayers that you can say for yourself, as well as poems to comfort and inspire you, Grace or Works not only asks you questions, it helps you make and maintain the right choices.

Book details:
Paperback: 122 pages
Language English
ISBN 978-0-9557898-5-4

 :www.protokospublishers.com

COMING OUT SOON

- GOOD DADS, BAD DADS.

- LET'S REASON TOGETHER - YOUTH'S A-Z.

USEFUL ADDRESSES:

Aglow International
Web site: www.aglow.org
Aglow International is a network of caring women, a faith-building organisation rooted in local groups and international in scope, yet one-on-one in ministry. Their mission is to lead women to Jesus Christ and provide opportunity for Christian women to grow in their faith and minister to others.

Care for the Family
PO Box 488
Cardiff
CF15 7YY
Tel: (029) 2081 0800
Fax: (029) 2081 4089
Email: mail@cff.org.uk
Web site: www.care-for-the-family.org.uk OR www.cff.org.uk
Care for the Family aims to promote strong family life and to help those hurting because of family breakdown. Their heart is to come alongside people in the good times and in the tough times – bringing hope, compassion and some practical, down-to-earth help and encouragement.

Focus on the Family
Tel: 1-800 - 232 6459
Web site: www.family.org
Focus on the Family cooperates with the Holy Spirit in disseminating the Gospel of Jesus Christ to as many people as possible, and, specifically, to accomplish that objective by helping to preserve traditional values and the institution of the family.

Protokos Publishers
www.protokospublishers.com - This site provides various resources for the family.

The Marriage Course
www.themarriagecourse.org
This site is for any couple who wants to invest in their relationship. They teach how to be happily married to the same person for a lifetime

Total Woman Ministries
3 Herringham Road
Thames Wharf Barrier,
Charlton,
London
SE7 8NJ.
Tel: 020 8293 3730
Fax: 020 8293 3731
Email: admin@totalwomanministries.org
Web site:www.totalwomanministries.org
Total Woman Ministries by God's grace has the sole vision of reaching out to women of all categories (married, single, separated / divorced, young, middle-aged or elderly).

To the Bride with Love

Dear Reader,

Thank you for your time and resources committed to supporting this writing ministry. Please help to tell others about how much the Lord has blessed you reading this book.

You will certainly be blessed by the other books written by Oluwakemi, so why not visit www.protokospublishers.com and place an order today.

It will equally be appreciated if you can help to write a few sentences review of the book on www.amazon.com and / or on www.protokospublishers.com.

Please note that all our books are easily available from our website.

God bless you as you do.
Management
Protokos Publishers.

www.ingramcontent.com/pod-product-compliance
Lightning Source LLC
Chambersburg PA
CBHW051450290426
44109CB00016B/1691